CHARLES DICKENS IN CHANCERY

BEING AN ACCOUNT OF HIS PROCEEDINGS IN RESPECT OF THE "CHRISTMAS CAROL" WITH SOME GOSSIP IN RELATION TO THE OLD LAW COURTS AT WESTMINSTER

BY

E. T. JAQUES

A SOLICITOR OF THE SUPREME COURT

THE LAWBOOK EXCHANGE, LTD.
Union, New Jersey
2001

ISBN 1-58477-106-2

Second printing 2005

Printed in the United States of America on acid-free paper

THE LAWBOOK EXCHANGE, LTD.
33 Terminal Avenue
Clark, New Jersey 07066-1321

Please see our website for a selection of our other publications and fine facsimile reprints of classic works of legal history:
www.lawbookexchange.com

Library of Congress Cataloging-in-Publication Data

Jaques, E. T. (Edward Tyrrell)
Charles Dickens in'Chancery: being an account of his proceedings in respect of the "Christmas carol" with some gossip in relation to the old law courts at Westminster / by E.T. Jaques.
p. cm.
ISBN 1-58477-106-2 (cloth: alk. paper)
1. Dickens, Charles, 1812-1870. Christmas carol. 2. Copyright--Great Britain--Cases.
I. Title.

PR4572.C69 J3 2000
823'.8--dc21

00-036238

CHARLES DICKENS IN CHANCERY

BEING AN ACCOUNT OF HIS PROCEEDINGS IN RESPECT OF THE "CHRISTMAS CAROL" WITH SOME GOSSIP IN RELATION TO THE OLD LAW COURTS AT WESTMINSTER

BY

E. T. JAQUES

A SOLICITOR OF THE SUPREME COURT

LONGMANS, GREEN AND CO.
39 PATERNOSTER ROW, LONDON
FOURTH AVENUE & 30TH STREET, NEW YORK
BOMBAY, CALCUTTA, AND MADRAS
1914

TO

EDWARD SHEARME, F.S.A.

SOMETIME A CHIEF CLERK TO THE VICE-CHANCELLOR MALINS

Charles Dickens in Chancery

THE *Christmas Carol* was published on the 19th of December 1843. Six thousand copies were sold on the first day, and before the end of 1844 the number had risen to fifteen thousand. For a book, costing five shillings and offering very little bulk for the money, this sale was enormous. There was, of course, the attraction of Leech's pictures, but taking the *Carol* as a whole, five shillings was a stiff price for the slim "foolscap octavo," with holly on the cover.

A sale of six thousand on the mere strength of a writer's name speaks volumes for his popularity. The new voice had made itself heard in *Pickwick*, some eight years earlier; and *Nickleby*, *Oliver Twist*, *The Old Curiosity Shop* and *Barnaby Rudge*, following in quick succession, had each attracted an ever-increasing audience. At thirty-one Charles Dickens was already a public character. His name was a household word wherever the English language was spoken; Edinburgh had feasted him and had made him a freeman of the City, and the American people had received him as their nation's guest.

By Christmas 1843 *Martin Chuzzlewit* in the original green covers had run more than half its course. The number for December had left old Martin under Pecksniff's roof, with that good man, "having Antony Chuzzlewit fresh in his recollection," watching with joyful expectancy the rapid progress of senile decay; the rupture with Tom Pinch was yet to come. Young Martin and Mark Tapley were luxuriating in the thriving city of Eden. Mrs. Gamp, fresh from the extraordinary experience of night-nursing pursued under conditions of wakefulness, had just dropped the most precious of her pearls—*But we never knows wot's hidden in each other's hearts; and if we had glass winders there, we'd need to keep the shetters up, some on us, I do assure you!*

Early in 1843 Dickens had presided at the opening of the Manchester Athenæum, and it was at Manchester that the fancy which ripened into the *Carol* had occurred to him. By the end of November the little book was written. "It was," says Forster, "the work of such odd moments of leisure as were left him out of the time taken up by two numbers of his *Chuzzlewit.*"

The ranks are thinning of those who know of their own knowledge what Dickens's books were to the people who read them as they came out; children of the fifties and the sixties cannot know this except by hearsay. It seems to me that he is the only author to whom our great non-literary public has ever given anything like the same attention which it always gives to politicians and notable criminals. Even Sir Walter was not master of a spell so far-reaching as this. The Scots as a nation knew him and were proud of him, but if the regiment of Lockhart's story had been raised south of the Border, the Laird of Abbotsford would never have been allowed to break the ranks. The story is so pretty that it will bear retelling, even here. On his way home from George the Fourth's coronation banquet, Sir Walter and a young friend got locked in the crowd, somewhere near Whitehall. The Scots Greys were keeping the roadway clear for privileged carriages, and the lame gentleman's appeal to be allowed to pass within the line, was met with a curt refusal—the sergeant's orders were strict; the thing was impossible. "*Take care, Sir Walter Scott: take care!*" exclaimed the young friend in a loud voice, as a new wave of turbulence threatened them from behind. "*What—Sir Walter Scott!*" quoth the sergeant: "*He shall get through anyhow!*" And through he went, the men echoing his name!

It would be a difficult and invidious task to analyse strictly the secret of Dickens's popularity with the classes to whom, notwithstanding our Education Acts, no other great writer makes any appeal. The primary reason admits of no doubt whatever—he was a genius, much of whose writing was devoted to homely things. But it would not be quite honest to ignore the fact that possibly the defects of his qualities—I have in mind the melodramatic character of many of his plots and incidents—may have swelled the number of his readers. This is a thorny subject, and any discussion of it would be out of place in these pages. I wish, however, to disclaim the suggestion that there is of necessity any connection between a writer's popularity and his merits, or that his influence bears any proportion to the number of his readers. There I may leave the matter. For present purposes I am not concerned with Dickens's merits ; and as regards his influence, I think it will be admitted on all hands that no one, literate or illiterate, can read him without being the better for it.

I was saying when I dropped my thread, that not even Scott was master of the spell which Dickens wielded. Seventy years ago, men gossiped about the new number of *Chuzzlewit* as they went to and from their business ; Pecksniff and Mrs. Gamp were discussed as if they were as real as the talkers' friends. At the present time no one but Sir Conan Doyle has invented a character whose name is familiar to all, and even in that case the knowledge of the man in the street goes no further than the fact that Sherlock Holmes was a solver of mysteries. He is not known as a human being at all. Only twice in my life have I overheard men chatting in a public place about a writer's characters as if they were flesh and blood. On the first occasion two Templars, dining at the Cock in Fleet Street, were discussing the newly-published *Jungle Book.* "Baloo was a thundering good chap," and so forth, was the burden of their song. On the second occasion a parson in a third-class carriage between Rochester and London waxed eloquent over *Puck*.

I suppose it will be pretty generally admitted that of living writers Mr. Kipling is the only one whose influence upon the national life is in any way comparable with that exercised by Dickens. He is in a sense heir to Dickens, as Dickens and Thackeray were co-heirs to Scott, and Scott was heir to Fielding. But though his influence upon letters and the world at large is greater than that of any of his brother authors, his works do not top the list of " best sellers " in the *Bookman's* reports. Certain dexterous blenders of piety and sexuality—so dexterous in some cases that we seem to see the author introducing his, or her, nastiness with the scrupulous judgment of a doctor prescribing strychnine—beat Mr. Kipling hollow. Dickens, however, had both popularity and influence in a measure to which the annals of literature can furnish no parallel: his books were " best sellers " and literary masterpieces as well. Bishops and judges revelled in them, and Forster tells us of a charwoman, so illiterate that she could not read, who in company with her fellow lodgers subscribed a penny a month, and held a monthly symposium at which the landlord of the house read aloud the new number of *Dombey and Son*.

Having now got back to Forster, I cannot do better than transcribe what he says about the reception of the *Christmas Carol*:—

> " Blessings on your kind heart," wrote Jeffrey . . . " you should be happy yourself, for you may be sure you have done more good by this little publication, fostered more kindly feelings, and prompted more positive acts of beneficence than can be traced to all the pulpits and confessionals in Christendom since Christmas 1842." " Who can listen," exclaimed Thackeray, " to objections regarding such a book as this ? It seems to me a national benefit, and to every man or woman who reads it a personal kindness." Such praise expressed what men of genius felt and said: but the small volume had other tributes, less

usual and not less genuine. There poured upon its author daily, all through that Christmas time, letters from complete strangers to him, which I remember reading with a wonder of pleasure; not literary at all, but of the simplest domestic kind, of which the general burden was to tell him, amid many confidences about their homes, how the *Carol* had come to be read aloud there and was to be kept upon a little shelf by itself, and was to do them no end of good. Anything more to be said of it will not add much to this.

A few pages earlier Forster has explained that the pecuniary result fell far short of Dickens's expectations. This, however, is a matter of no importance to anybody now; and after all, the first year's profit was nearly eight hundred pounds.

One of the penalties which Dickens had to pay for his enormous popularity was the shameless way in which his copyright was infringed by the issue of cheap colourable imitations of his stories. In many cases these piracies were little less than abbreviated reprints of his text. The hack dramatists, too, seized upon him as their prey. Readers of the *Life* would suppose that the performance of garbled versions of the novels was a serious irritation to Dickens, but it seems pretty clear from Edmund Yates's *Recollections and Experiences* that Forster has somewhat exaggerated his friend's annoyance as regards theatrical adaptations. Lawyers were generally of opinion that the playwrights' thefts were legal, and Dickens as a reasonable man took things much as he found them. Provided the kept dramatists waited until a story was finished, he did not greatly trouble himself about their productions; there is evidence, indeed, that on one occasion he so much enjoyed an adaptation of his *Nickleby* that he contemplated seeing the play a second time.

And apart from the fact that the law was supposed to give no remedy, another consolation was open to him: in those days, when minor dramatists had to accept ten shillings an act, the remuneration of playwrights was at best so small that

Dickens was not seriously injured in pocket by other men putting his creatures upon the stage. With the piratical reprints of his books the case was different. Here the injury to his pocket was serious. Whether it was so serious as he thought it, is a question which no one can settle now. As hereafter appears, one printer swore that at least seventy thousand copies of some of the penny numbers of his piratical magazine had been circulated, but I am inclined to doubt whether any of his purchasers would have bought the genuine Dickens. A small proportion of them, however, might have got the books from circulating libraries, thereby increasing the author's sales.

The pirates had been at work ever since *Pickwick* had made Dickens the most popular writer of the day, but he did nothing but rage and grumble until the *Carol* fell into their clutches. Then his wrath boiled over. Forster tells the story thus:

> Another and graver wrong [than the unauthorised dramatization of his books] was the piracy of his writings, every one of which had been reproduced with merely such colourable changes of title, incidents, and names of characters, as were believed to be sufficient to evade the law and adapt them to penny purchasers. So shamelessly had this been going on ever since the days of *Pickwick*, in so many outrageous ways and with all but impunity, that a course repeatedly urged by Talfourd and myself was at last taken . . . with the *Christmas Carol* and *Chuzzlewit* pirates.

Forster goes on to narrate the result of these proceedings; but from first to last he says very little about them. He even omits the names of the defendants, and to the best of my belief, no other writer upon Dickens has touched the subject. A good many years ago it occurred to me that it might be worth while to search the files of the Court and ascertain the details. This I have now done. *The Times* of 1844 furnished me with the name of one of the causes in which Dickens figured as plaintiff, and with this clue in my hands, I have been able to follow the litigation from start to finish. So complete are our Chancery records, and so well are they indexed at the Public Record Office, that the task has been mere child's play.

And having got thus far, let me confess that it is with some prickings of conscience that as a result of these searches I put forward my present addition to the mass of writing about Dickens which the last quarter of a century has brought forth—a mass which in the opinion of some good judges is fairly comparable with Mr. Boffin's dust heaps. I have an uncomfortable suspicion that writing of this kind encourages the present-day tendency to read about an author, rather than to read his books; and I know that in the case of Dickens the flood of comment and gossip has already passed all bounds. Nothing in any way connected with him has been thought too trivial for the public eye. Not many years ago, one of the items of a "Dickens Exhibition" was a shirt-collar, formerly owned—and presumably worn—by the object of this idolatry. It was an ignominious and repulsive thing. Grimy with the dust of many years, it might have come from the neck of Mr. Smangle himself. To some of us a certain glass-case at Abbotsford is none too pleasant an object, but there is a wide gulf between the garments there displayed and a very dirty collar.

Much ink has been spent upon the elucidation and discussion of small matters of biography, ignored or scarcely mentioned by Forster. But facts, however petty, are not without their value, and a strict winnowing of this chaff may afford material for a few additional pages of the *Life*. Fact, however, bears a very small proportion of the mass of writing which the present Dickens worship has produced. Questions whether this house, or that house, was the actual building which he had in his mind when he described the habitation of one of his characters, have been exhaustively debated on both sides of the Atlantic. Whole books have been written upon *Edwin Drood*, some of them advocating a theory so degrading to Dickens as an artist that it makes the gorge rise. The scope of our investigators knows no limit. If the great man's laundress were ascertainable, who can doubt that her reminiscences would be duly chronicled, and that her portrait, and pictures of her residence and wash-tub, would figure in the newspapers?

I am not entitled to speak with any real severity of these labours, for I have had my full share of them. In all humility be it confessed that it was I, and no other, who identified No. 54 Hatton Garden as the Police Office of *Oliver Twist*,[1] who pointed out that the Dog and Pot was still on view in the Blackfriars Road,[2] who adduced evidence tending to show that the clerkship to Molloy was after the clerkship in Gray's Inn,[3] who searched the Marshalsea register and found out the exact term of John Dickens's imprisonment,[4] to say nothing of at least one excursion into regions of pure fancy of the kind above referred to.

So far, however, my contributions to the so-called "Dickens literature" have been trifling in bulk, but now that I am devoting a whole booklet to so small an incident of the man's career as his attempt to protect a copyright, my conscience is not altogether at rest. Still, the defence raised by the pirates throws a strange light upon the byways of letters seventy years ago, and the proceedings are in my opinion so closely connected with *Bleak House* that I think they are worth recalling; and even at the risk of being more futile than my brethren, I have decided to tell the story. The fact that at one time Dickens was inclined to publish the affidavits as an appendix to *Chuzzlewit* is, of itself, some excuse for my venture. I

[1] *Chambers's Journal*, May 1902.

[2] *Temple Bar*, October 1903.

[3] *Pall Mall Gazette*, 10th February 1912.

[4] *Pall Mall Gazette*, 17th November 1910, and *Athenæum*, 9th November 1911. The evidence furnished by the Marshalsea register throws so much new light upon the most painful episode of Dickens's childhood, that I have thought well to deal with it in a note at the end of the Appendix.

can also plead that, so far as I know, the ground is quite untrodden.

Perhaps an apology is due to my non-legal readers for the space which I have devoted to the old Law Courts at Westminster. My original intention was to ascertain where Dickens's judge sat, and to ignore the rest of the buildings. But the search proved somewhat troublesome; and by the time it was completed, I had incidentally learned so much about the Courts as a whole, and had expended so much labour in the process, that I thought it would be a pity not to put my gleanings upon record. It is only in scraps, here, there, and everywhere, so to speak, that information about these Courts can be obtained. The explanation is simple enough—they were commonplace in themselves; they were not in the least venerable, and the glamour of association is a plant of slow growth. When Foss wrote a paper on the Legal History of Westminster Hall he did not condescend to notice the Courts then in use. That was in 1866, but even now they are too near our own day to excite any interest. The next generation, however, may be asking where they used to stand, and I am not without hope that the information which I have got together, trivial though it be, may prove useful to some future writer, when the time comes for associating Soane's buildings with the famous trials held therein, and the famous actors who played their parts upon the stage which those trials furnished. In this connection I wish to express my thanks to Mr. W. J. R. Pochin, of Gray's Inn, for the information which he has given me upon certain points connected with the Rolls, and for putting me upon inquiry as regards other matters.

I have said above that the task of searching the records proved to be mere child's play, but at the beginning it threatened to be so serious that I was half-inclined to abandon it forthwith. The index of Chancery orders for Hilary Term 1844 disclosed the fact that Dickens was then plaintiff in no less than four

Chancery suits. This was a good deal more than I had bargained for. But I made a plunge by calling for the court copy of the first of the orders disclosed by this index; and when in response to a shilling application-form, a huge volume was laid before me, it proved to contain a copy of all the four; and ten-minutes' inspection satisfied me that though separate defendants, or sets of defendants, had been proceeded against, the relief sought for, and granted, had in every case been the same. The four orders were identical, except as regards the names, addresses, and descriptions of the defendants, and they all bore date the 11th of January 1844. This was a good shilling's worth; and I pursued my labours like a giant refreshed.

Before long I came upon a fifth suit, in which an order had been made on the 10th of January. These proceedings turned out to be by far the most important of all, inasmuch as the defendants had shown fight and had raised on affidavit a defence which ought to have landed some of them at the Old Bailey to answer an indictment for perjury.

I will not weary the reader with a description of the steps whereby I obtained a full knowledge of the litigation so briefly referred to by Forster. I will merely state as simply as I can what Dickens complained of when he went into Chancery, and how he fared when he got there.

The old Chancery procedure by bill and answer, the bill being the plaintiff's statement of his case and the defendant's answer being what its name implies, continued down to the 1st of November 1875. The defendants to Dickens's five bills were as follows:

(1) Richard Egan Lee and John Haddock, of Craven Yard, Drury Lane, booksellers and publishers.

(2) George Berger, of 19 Holywell Street, bookseller and publisher.

(3) John Cleave, of Shoe Lane, bookseller and publisher.

(4) William Strange, of 21 Paternoster Row, bookseller and publisher, and

(5) William Mark Clark, of 17 Warwick Lane, bookseller and publisher.

The main suit was that against Lee and Haddock, they having procured and published the piratical version of the *Carol*, which was the subject-matter of all the proceedings. None of the other defendants showed fight. In these circumstances I will tell the story as the same is revealed by the file in *Dickens* v. *Lee*.

The bill of complaint against Lee and Haddock is a tremendous document. Engrossed in a fair clerkly hand upon two skins of parchment, it contains about three thousand words, and is signed by James Bacon, the counsel who settled it. It was pleasant to come upon his name, for when I was young I saw much of this James Bacon. He made such an impression on my youthful mind that shortly after his death I wrote a sketch of him in the *St. James's Gazette*,[1] and later on I introduced him into a story called *The Vice-Chancellor's Ward*. When I used to study him he was the last of the vice-chancellors, and an old gentleman of very marked individuality. Deaf he was, and sometimes inclined to be crusty; but even on the verge of ninety his mind was as clear as spring water, and his command of the English language was the admiration of his contemporaries. I saw him take his farewell of the Bench on the 10th of November 1886, nine months after he had attained his eighty-eighth year. Whether any man ought to be a judge at that age is an open question; but looking back across the gap of time which separates us from the eighties, and recalling the old vice-chancellor and his ways, I verily believe that notwithstanding his testiness and a disinclination to go an inch further into anything than he thought necessary, he was a competent judge to the very end. He had his likes and dislikes as regards the men practising

[1] This article is reprinted in Mr. Edward Manson's *Builders of our Law under Queen Victoria*.

before him ; and this fact, coupled with a gift of phrasing, made him something of a terror to the Bar. But he was fair and just at bottom, and in his time Chancery Court I was a very different place from the sink of favouritism to which one of his successors degraded it. Sir James Bacon lived to be over ninety-seven. He was infirm of body long before he retired, but it was only at the very end that his intellect failed him. More than seventy years before his death he had been a friend of Charles and Mary Lamb. In Miss Sichel's *Life* of Canon Ainger there is a letter about them written when he was ninety-two : a beautiful little bit of retrospect, embellished with an exquisite and most felicitous quotation from *Macbeth.*

The bill of complaint which he settled in *Dickens* v. *Lee* stated that " the orator "—for so a Chancery plaintiff was called in those days—had invented and written the *Christmas Carol,* and that in the sixteenth number of a periodical work called *Parley's Illuminated Library* the defendants had published a colourable imitation of about one half of this book ; and the bill went on to ask for an injunction to restrain them from " printing, publishing, selling, or otherwise disposing of the said publication, or any continuation thereof." Dickens's solicitor was Thomas Mitton, then practising at 23 Southampton Buildings, Chancery Lane.

On the 10th of January 1844—the day after the filing of the bill—Bacon on Dickens's behalf applied to Vice-Chancellor Knight Bruce for what is called an interim injunction. This application was made *ex parte : i.e.* in the absence of the defendants and without notice to them. It must have been quick work to get the bill filed and the evidence in support of the application ready so soon, for No. 16 of *Parley's Illuminated Library* had not been published until Saturday the 6th of January.

The evidence, other than a formal certificate of the due filing of the bill, consisted of an affidavit of Dickens and an affidavit of Mitton's clerk. A full copy of these is printed in the Appendix hereto, but I must state their purport as I go on, or the thread of my story will be broken.

Charles Dickens of 1 *Devonshire Terrace, York Gate, Regents Park, in the Parish of St. Marylebone, in the County of Middlesex, says:*

He is the author of several books. Before the preceding December, he wrote the *Christmas Carol*, a work of invention and fancy, and the sole right of printing and publishing it is in him. The book was published on the 19th of December. It immediately became extremely popular, and is of great value to the deponent. The defendants have made, or procured to be made, a colourable imitation. They have already printed or published a part of same, entitled *A Christmas Ghost Story, reoriginated from the original by Charles Dickens, Esquire, and analytically condensed expressly for this work*, such part purporting to be No. 16 of *Parley's Illuminated Library*, published on the 6th of January. This number contains a colourable imitation of about one-half of the *Christmas Carol*, and is a mere piracy of same; the subject, characters, personages, and incidents being taken from and being the same as those of the *Christmas Carol*, except that the name "Fezziwig" has been altered to "Fuzziwig." Though in many instances the language of the book has been altered, all such alteration is only colourable, and has been made for the purpose of endeavouring to conceal the fact that the deponent's work has been copied, or imitated. The deponent having first become acquainted with the said piracy at 3 o'clock on Saturday, the 6th of January, he on the following Monday, instructed his solicitor to apply for an injunction. The deponent firmly believes, and is fully persuaded, that the defendants intend to publish the residue of the *Christmas Carol*, unless restrained by the order of the Court.

Robert Bach, clerk to Thomas Mitton, of 23 *Southampton Buildings, in the County of Middlesex, solicitor for the plaintiff, says:*

On the 8th of January he purchased at the shop of the defendants in Craven Yard, Drury Lane, in the County of

> Middlesex, No. 16 of *Parley's Illuminated Library,* which is a colourable imitation of about one-half of the *Christmas Carol,* and is a mere piracy of that book; the subject, characters, personages, and incidents of the two books being the same, except that "Fezziwig" of the *Christmas Carol* is called "Fuzziwig" in the *Christmas Ghost Story.* In an exhibited copy of the *Christmas Ghost Story* the deponent has underscored, and marked in the margin, several of the passages which follow the language of the *Carol,* and in all other parts the incidents and characters of the two books are the same and follow in the same order.

When I came upon Dickens's affidavit, I hoped that it would show some traces of his composition, but the language proved to be so technical that I had no hesitation in attributing the sole authorship to Bacon. But after all, the signature is Dickens's, and this gives the document a living interest. The flourish with its many curls is a particularly fine specimen of his handiwork.

Bacon's application was successful. The order made, omitting only a long recital of the evidence, is set out in the Appendix, from which it will be seen that Knight Bruce restrained the defendants from printing, publishing, selling, or otherwise disposing of their piratical instalment of the *Carol,* or any continuation thereof. It seems probable that this order was made at the vice-chancellor's residence. It is a vacation order, and the registrar's books show that his Honour made no other between the 22nd of December and the 11th of January. If Bacon and Mitton had to take a jaunt to Roehampton where Knight Bruce lived, Mr. Registrar Hussey must have done likewise, for his minute bears internal evidence that it was made in the vice-chancellor's presence, and was not merely copied from the endorsement upon counsel's brief.

To the modern Chancery eye, this order is a very cumbersome document. There is nothing particularly archaic about the language of the operative part; it is the setting out of the contents of the two affidavits which seems so superfluous. At the present day an *ex parte* order for injunction contains something not appearing in the old form, namely the plaintiff's undertaking in damages, but the total length rarely exceeds four or five hundred words, whereas Mr. Registrar Hussey employed nearly two thousand.

Next day—the 11th of January, and the first day of Hilary Term—a similar order was made on motion in each of the four other suits. On these motions Bacon was led by Talfourd, then a serjeant of ten-years' standing. Considerations of etiquette had probably forbidden his appearance on the 10th of January, before the vice-chancellor in private.

These four orders were made at Westminster, for seventy years ago the equity courts still sat there in term time. I am satisfied that these sittings, except on ceremonial occasions, had been discontinued by the end of the fifties, but I cannot say when the change was made.[1] Only those who have looked into questions of this kind can have any notion of how difficult they are to solve. The evidence lurks in all sorts of places—Acts of Parliament and legal memoirs, for instance—but unless he be exceptionally lucky, the searcher may waste hours over a trumpery point, and find himself no wiser in the end.

The Times shows that on the 11th of January 1844 all five chancery judges then in existence, namely the Lord Chancellor, the Master of the Rolls, the Vice-Chancellor of England, and the two additional vice-chancellors were sitting at Westminster. When in 1820 Soane planned his buildings, it was only necessary to assign courts to the Chancellor and the Vice-Chancellor of England, for the additional vice-chancellors were not created until 1841, and the Master of the

[1] "... at the earnest request of the counsel and solicitors the Lord Chancellor consented to sit in Lincoln's Inn during one or more terms in each year, and the convenience of this proved so great that the sittings of the Courts of Equity are now entirely held in the latter place." Pamphlet: *Observations on the proposed Concentration of the Courts of Justice*, London, Spottiswoode, 1859, p. 4.

Rolls always sat at the Rolls House in Chancery Lane. Nine years later, however, he began to sit at Westminster, and a large room on the first floor was adapted to his use.

In passing, one may mention the curious fact that though the judicial status of the Master of the Rolls was fully recognised so far back as the reign of Henry VIII, he was, down to 1829, regarded as the Lord Chancellor's vice or deputy, and as such he never sat when the Chancellor was sitting. For this reason the court hours of the Rolls were from six to ten in the evening. On the 22nd of June 1829 the Master of the Rolls sat for the first time at Westminster, and thenceforth the night sittings were discontinued. I have in the Appendix set forth certain extracts from *The Times* announcing the change, and reporting the first sitting under the new conditions.[1]

The Act of 1841 appointing the two additional vice-chancellors made a further demand upon Soane's buildings, and two more upper rooms—one on the first floor, and the other on the second —were brought into requisition. These were called the First

[1] Apart from *The Times* extracts set out in the Appendix (pp. 91, 92), my authorities for the statements contained in this paragraph are the following: *Discourse on the Judicial Authority of the Master of the Rolls* (1727); Foss's *Judges*, vol. v. p. 4; *Enc. Britt.* (11th Ed.), article, "Master of the Rolls," and *Enc. of the Laws of England*, vol. ix. p. 80. In both encyclopædias the date of the change is erroneously given as 1827. It is right in the *Dict. Nat. Biog.*, article, "Sir John Leach." These late sittings had not always been peculiar to the Rolls; it appears by Campbell's *Lives of the Chancellors*, ch. cxl., that at the beginning of the reign of George III the Court of Chancery sat on Wednesday and Friday evenings, and that the king at Lord Northington's request allowed the practice to be discontinued. Presumably there had been no contemporaneous sittings of the Rolls. Campbell goes on to say that when Sir William Grant was Master of the Rolls, he dined—"with a bottle of Madeira and a bottle of port"—at ten o'clock, after the rising of his court. For the encouragement of my teetotal readers, I may as well add that he died in his eightieth year. It will be understood that the night sittings above referred to were not special in their nature, or occasioned by a press of work, or a desire to clear the paper, but were part of the ordinary routine. Eldon and Brougham, to say nothing of other judges who may have done the same, both sat late upon occasions. In Romilly's *Diary* he mentions, under date of the 23rd of August 1811, that for a week Eldon had been sitting from nine to four in the morning, and from half-past five till ten in the evening. This he did to clear off a mass of bankruptcy petitions.

and Second Vice-Chancellor's Courts. The upper one was generally known as the "Cockloft." This I never saw, but I well remember that the First Vice-Chancellor's Court was what our forefathers called a "dog-hole." Here, no doubt, Knight Bruce, as the senior of the two additional vice-chancellors, had his seat, and here he heard the motion in *Dickens* v. *Lee*.

More than thirty years have gone by since the old Courts passed into disuse, and the greater part of the land on which they stood is now green lawns dominated by a statue of the Lord Protector. But so many of my legal readers will recall the general features as the same existed in 1882, that I think they will like to be reminded of the details.

In 1820 the Courts of Chancery and King's Bench occupied respectively the south-west and south-east corners of the Hall. The Bail Court lay beyond the east wall, and was, I think, approached by an entrance a little north of the King's Bench. The site of the proposed new Courts was the oblong space lying between Westminster Hall and St. Margaret Street, then covered by a mass of old buildings comprising the Court of Common Pleas, the two Courts of Exchequer, various offices devoted to the storage of records, and in the south-west corner, certain rooms appurtenant to the House of Commons. Tradition says part of these old buildings was used as the royal lodgings when the Palace of Westminster was still a residence of the sovereign.

Soane managed to find space for all the courts under one roof. They were nearly finished early in 1824, but a storm rose in the House of Commons, with the result that a Select Committee was appointed to inspect and revise his work. In the end, part of it was rebuilt according to a new plan, and it was not until 1828 that the structure was completed. Except as regards certain alterations of detail in the upper floors, Soane's Courts underwent no change until they were pulled down in, or about, 1884.

Beginning at the north end of Westminster Hall, the first was the King's Bench. This lay some 30 or 40 feet west of the corridor which ran along the whole length of the Hall, and formed a vestibule to the courts adjoining. It was in the King's (then the Queen's) Bench that the trial at bar of the Tichborne Claimant was held, and the legal traditions of the ground on which it stood went back to the early Henries. The Great Court of Exchequer—built no one knows when, but undoubtedly altered, or reconstructed, by Elizabeth—was at the north end of Soane's oblong. He meant to preserve this fine court, but he was too late. Roughly speaking, it extended from New Palace Yard for 46 feet towards the south, and for that distance it filled up more than two-thirds of the space between Westminster Hall and St. Margaret Street. Inderwick—on what authority I know not—says that Elizabeth sometimes used it as a ball-room. It is easy enough to map out the site as one stands in St. Margaret Street—the present Grand Committee Room covers a part of it—but not so easy to recall the atmosphere of a time when royal balls could be held in a Court of Justice, with Gloriana and her Chancellor among the dancers. It is curious to think that Gray's sportive reference to Hatton may have been literally true if applied to that Great Court—

> "Full oft within the spacious walls
> When he had fifty winters o'er him
> My grave Lord-Keeper led the brawls :
> The seals and maces danced before him."

Few of those who tread the roadway between Westminster Hall and St. Margaret's Church know anything of the memories attaching to the ground under their feet. Edward the Confessor's Palace of Westminster stood south of the present Hall, but the Palace of Rufus covered the site upon which Soane's Courts were built. I have set forth in the Appendix certain references to Elizabeth's connection with the buildings which Soane replaced, including the mention of a tradition that an upper chamber close to the north-west tower of the Hall was Edward the Sixth's nursery. Readers of Froude will feel no doubt that Henry VIII was often in that room. The temptation to say more about the old Palace of Westminster is strong; but space forbids, and I must go back to Soane's buildings.

At the east end of the passage which led from the corridor above mentioned to the King's Bench was the Bail Court. Next to the Bail Court was the Exchequer. Behind this was the Exchequer Chamber, which after the abolition of its old Equity jurisdiction by the Act creating the two additional Vice-Chancellors, was used for the hearing of appeals. South of the Exchequer proper was the Common Pleas. Here the civil action of *Tichborne* v. *Lushington* was tried. Next to the Common Pleas came the Vice-Chancellor of England's Court, generally known within living memory as the Lords Justices' Court. The next and last was the Court of Chancery, otherwise the Lord Chancellor's Court. Beyond this was a retiring room, 28 feet long by 16 feet wide),[1] designed for the Chancellor, and afterwards used by the judges appointed under the Probate and Divorce Acts of 1857).[2] Readers of *Bleak House* will remember that it was in the Court of Chancery at Westminster that *Jarndyce* v. *Jarndyce* came to an end.

On the first floor of Soane's buildings, somewhat in rear of the Vice-Chancellor's Court and the Court of Chancery, was the Rolls, and near this on the same level was the First Vice-Chancellor's Court, with the "Cockloft" on the floor above. A passage ran out at the south-west corner of the Hall just beyond the Chancellor's retiring-room. From this passage a staircase gave public access to the three upper Courts.

It must not be forgotten that down to the general removal from Westminster, the first day of Michaelmas Term in each year saw

[1] Britton and Pugin's *Illustrations of the Public Buildings of London* (1828), vol. ii. p. 259.

[2] Pamphlet: *Observations on the proposed Concentration of the Courts of Justice* (Spottiswoode, 1859), p. 4.

most of the Chancery judges back in their old Courts. On the 2nd of November 1882 the judges walked up Westminster Hall for the last time. On that occasion Bacon sat in the Lords Justices' Court, Chitty in the Rolls, and Kay in the First Vice-Chancellor's Court. Except on this one day in each November—I am writing, be it understood, of the last years of the old Courts—Sir Robert Phillimore tried Admiralty cases in the Rolls, and the First and Second Vice-Chancellor's Courts were used by one Division or another as occasion required. In June 1879 I attended a trial before Mr. Justice Lindley and a common jury in the First Vice-Chancellor's Court. The action was for slander, and the present Attorney-General for the Duchy of Lancaster was the defendant's counsel. The place was so small that when Mr. McCall warmed up to his work, the volume of his youthful eloquence was almost overpowering.

Probably the Lords Justices' Court was assigned to Bacon at the last sitting of the Chancery judges at Westminster, in order to spare him an ascent to the first floor; but seeing that the court had been built for the Vice-Chancellor of England, and that in November 1882 Sir James was the sole survivor of all the Vice-Chancellors, it was singularly appropriate that he should have been its last Chancery occupant. The old man was present at the opening of the Royal Courts by Queen Victoria on the 4th of the following December. *The Times* says that he walked up Street's hall, "the last of his rank, in a distinctive robe of blue with a profusion of gold lace."

All the world knew the old courts, but the region that lay between them and the roadway which passes St. Margaret's church was private. Much of this space was occupied by the judges' quarters and the bar robing-rooms; and at the extreme south-west corner, near Old Palace Yard, was a library, originally assigned to the Masters in Chancery. There was some family life in the upper part of these back premises. House-keepers and the like had their homes in rooms that looked across to St. Margaret's church, and here people were born and died. The private approaches to the Courts were all on this west side. There were four, or five, so-called "Judges' Entrances"; and running past the Chancery Library was an entrance sacred to the Lord Chancellor.

No judge now on the bench ever sat in the old Courts, and of all the minor officials, male and female, who migrated to Temple Bar in 1882, I have been able to find only three still on duty. The recollection of the oldest of these goes back to the early fifties, when Campbell was Lord Chief Justice. The people who passed their lives in that part of Soane's buildings which was hidden from the public eye were a close corporation, whereof everyone knew all about his neighbours, and not a little about the august figures in silk and ermine whose satellites they were. This small world could hold its tongue, and the same reticence is observable in the few that yet survive. But bygone days at Westminster are dear to those who passed their youth there; and now and again as I talked with these survivors, a gleam of memory of things personal would light up the dry details of my investigation: perhaps a casual reference to somebody, long dead, who had owned a vested interest in one of the robing-rooms; a mention of Campbell's imposing presence, or Cockburn's beautiful voice and the rolling character of his walk. Trivial incidents of the daily round came back in all their freshness: intimate trifles like the small chop which was Hannen's usual lunch in his pre-vegetarian days; the winter fire that blazed in the judges' hall; and the bench which was cut to accommodate a Lord Justice's swelling port. Trifles indeed, but something more to those who recalled them! Not far removed from tears was the emotion of one survivor, as she dwelt upon the life which had throbbed about the old Courts, and assured me that when, nowadays, she saw the cleared space and realised how small it was, she could hardly believe that the past had not been all a dream.

Westminster Hall was the seat of justice for nearly eight hundred years, but Soane's Courts were not in existence for much more than half a century. Now, not one stone remains upon another, and before long all recollection of them will have passed away. But the Courts at Temple Bar are on quite another footing. They are built for eternity, and it seems a pity that something cannot be done to keep alive the memories of the last thirty years, to say nothing of the days that are yet to be. Owing to recent changes, and the re-numbering and re-naming consequent thereupon, it may not be easy a few years hence to say where the Parnell Commission sat; and who will remember that Chancery Court III of to-day was originally the Lord Chancellor's Court? A brass plate, no bigger than a visiting card, would hold a name, and this screwed into the bench, or a panel, would for all time associate a judge with the court in which he sat. Many of the records would be names, and nothing more, soon after the men had passed away, but—to mention only two of the judges whom my generation holds in reverence—I would fain believe that posterity will wish to know where Chitty and Sir James Stirling used to sit.

Inderwick's *The King's Peace* (1895) contains a copy of Soane's plan of Westminster Hall and its surroundings in 1795. A plan by J. T. Smith, dated 1807, is given in that writer's *Antiquities of the City of Westminster*, 1807. Plans and pictures of Soane's Courts, with certain letterpress describing the woes inflicted upon the architect, will be found in his *Brief Statement of the Proceedings respecting the New Law Courts at Westminster*, 1828. There are pictures of the Courts of Chancery and King's Bench, with some general descriptive matter, in Britton and Pugin's *Illustrations of the Public Buildings of London* (1828), vol. ii. There is a plan of Westminster Palace, including the Hall and the Law Courts, in Brayley and Britton's *History of the Ancient Palace . . . at Westminster* (1836), facing p. 447, and a woodcut of the Lord Chancellor's Court is given in Knight's *London* (1851), vol. vi. p. 385. My statements as to the uses to which some of the Courts were put in later years are founded, as to part, on oral evidence obtained from the three members of the Royal Courts of Justice staff above referred to, supplemented by my own recollection, and as to the rest, on information furnished by (1) the pamphlet cited in the footnote to p. 19 ; (2) a file of *The Times*, and (3) certain issues of the *Law List* and other periodical publications.

A pretty full report of the hearing of the motion for interim injunction in Dickens's suits against the four booksellers appears in *The Times* of the 12th of January 1844. This is printed in the Appendix, and it is not necessary to give any extracts here. I thought it worth while to consult the registrar's book in the hope of finding some further particulars. This hope was somewhat faint, for certain researches which, years ago, I made into the books of Lord Eldon's registrars, when I was trying to get to the bottom of the famous litigation in respect of Drury Lane Theatre, had proved to be a mere waste of time. All the record I found of Sheridan's speeches was the bare entry of his name. Incidentally I came upon something interesting—a manuscript of Eldon's monumental Judgment in *Sibley* v. *Perry*, copied apparently by Mr. Registrar Coppinger from the Chancellor's draft—but I had to journey to the Museum and consult the *Morning Chronicle* before I could find out how the Drury Lane proceedings had gone.

I think that searchers of the books of our later registrars will get a better reward for their labours. The late Germain Lavie—a bright spirit quenched, alas, too soon!—used to record upon his note any good thing, or touch of character, which had cast a gleam of humour upon the day's routine, and I doubt not that the Latin epigrams, which he knocked off so easily and with so much enjoyment as he sat in court, were all drafted on the margin of his book. I do not suggest that the parchment-clad volumes of his brethren will be found to contain matter of this sort, for Lavie shone with a brilliancy all his own, but I feel sure that the registrars of to-day are less sparing of their ink than their predecessors used to be. And though I have already wandered a long way from my subject, I will venture to add a question, in the hope that it may meet some sympathetic eye on the other side of the Border—have Sir Walter's minute-books ever been looked through? Surely the ready pen which gossiped so delightfully in the *Journal* must have sometimes dropped a pearl upon the court record.

The note made by Wood, one of Knight Bruce's registrars, was not amiss, but it was not adorned with any marginalia. All that I learned from it, beyond what was shown on the face of the orders, was the fact that his Honour had disposed of thirty-six matters before Talfourd moved, and that the court rose as soon as the last of the Dickens motions had been heard.

So far as my knowledge of the record extends, these interim orders were the end of the proceedings against the four minor offenders. Probably negotiations followed between these defendants and Mitton, and I dare say their unsold stocks of the *Christmas Ghost Story* were delivered up, or destroyed. But any such arrangement as this may well have been come to entirely out of court.

That these humbler pirates should have struck their flag was natural enough; the marvel is that the printers should have ventured to show fight. The case against them was so black that in the normal course of things they would have accepted the injunction—thunderbolt though it probably was!—as one of the calamities of life, no more to be revoked than death itself. But fight they did! Whether as the law stood in 1844 the charge of laches and acquiescence which they made against Dickens in respect of their earlier piracies gave them a real fighting chance, I cannot say. No doubt they were advised that the point was arguable; and this, coupled with the knowledge that if they were unable to fly the Jolly Roger, they could no longer carry on their business, decided them to find money for counsel and solicitor, and make a desperate attempt to get the injunction dissolved. Dickens never got a penny out of them towards his costs, but unless their solicitor, Mr. William Henry Cross, of 28 Surrey Street, Strand, and Barnes, Surrey, had a particularly trustful disposition, and—unlike Mr. Voles—he was a man of capital, he must have drawn a fair sum on account before he filed five affidavits and instructed a leader and a junior on Messrs. Lee and Haddock's behalf.

Endless are the gibes which have been lavished upon affidavit evidence, and any old Chancery hand can recall instances of this form of perjury every bit as gross as the classical examples ; but having carefully studied the defendants' evidence in *Dickens* v. *Lee* I venture to doubt whether, " even in an affidavit," the truth has ever been handled more carelessly. And the form and language of the documents is such that the inference that they were settled by counsel is irresistible !

Haddock lay low and said nothing, but Lee came forward as a deponent, and he was backed up by the oaths of the so-called author of the *Christmas Ghost Story*, the artist who illustrated it, and two literary men who swore that the charge of piracy was wholly unfounded. A copy of this evidence is printed in the Appendix, and the main points are set out below.

Richard Egan Lee, of Craven Yard, St. Clement Danes, in the County of Middlesex, printer and publisher, the managing partner of the firm of Lee and Haddock, says :

> He did, in conjunction with his coadjutor, Mr. Henry Hewitt, a gentleman of considerable experience and talent, analyse, complete, and publish nine volumes of *Parley's Library, or Treasury of Knowledge, Entertainment, and Delight.* In the first volume his coadjutor did analyse, abridge, reoriginate and publish *The Old Curiosity Shop* and *Barnaby Rudge*, and did dedicate that volume to Dickens. Seventy thousand at least of some parts of the said volume were printed and published. A copy of the said volume bearing the deponent's autograph

inscription was, before Christmas 1841, transmitted to Dickens, who never in any way interfered to prevent the publication or circulation thereof. In execution of the express purpose of *Parley's Library*—namely to impart in a familiar style synoptical sketches of all works of value, both ancient and modern—some of Dickens's other productions have been analysed and reproduced therein, while others, deemed by the deponent and his coadjutor to be of unequal and inferior merit and pretentions, have not been noticed at all. Beside the Plaintiff's works, books of Joanna Baillie, Mrs. Gore, Captain Marryat, Sir Edward Lytton Bulwer, Lord Byron, Moore, Lockhart, Campbell, Cooper, James, Warren, and very many other distinguished writers have been in like manner systematically, and as the deponent verily believes, honestly and fairly reoriginated by close analysis and condensation of plot and incident, and no complaint has been made. Soon after the publication of the *Christmas Carol*, the deponent, in the exercise of his usual avocations, and in accordance with the general custom of editors, critically examined that work, and his opinion and the notes which he made were communicated to Mr. Hewitt, who proceeded to abridge and analytically condense the book; and who by the exercise of much skill, talent, and invention, reoriginated the same in brief. After having critically examined Mr. Hewitt's manuscript, the deponent had three illustrations prepared by one George Stiff, an artist of great reputation and distinguished talent. In the deponent's opinion, and indeed, as he meant to express when he penned the title of the reproduction, very considerable improvements and large original additions, as well as condensations, have been effected by Mr. Hewitt: for example, where in the *Christmas Carol* Tiny Tim is merely described as having sung a song, Mr. Hewitt has written a song of sixty lines, such song being admirably adapted to the occasion and replete with pathos and poetry. So far from the *Christmas Ghost Story* being a colourable imitation of the plaintiff's book, numerous incongruities in the *Carol*, involving the unhinging of the whole plot, have been tastefully remedied by Mr. Hewitt's extended critical experience of dramatic effect, and his ready perception of harmonies. To Mr. Hewitt's writing the plaintiff is indebted for the germs of many of his works; the original suggestion for the *Carol* itself having been first derived from *Parley's Library*.

A considerable outlay of money was required to produce the *Christmas Ghost Story*. The next number of *Parley's Library* ought to, and should, and would, have been published on the 13th of January if the injunction had not been granted. The actual loss and damage occasioned by the injunction amounts to a serious and considerable sum, and deponent solemnly avers that unless such injunction be forthwith dissolved, the pecuniary loss to him and his partner will be ruinous and absolutely irreparable.

Henry Hewitt, of 101 *White Lion Street, Islington, in the County of Middlesex, author and editor, says :*

He has for thirty-five years been engaged in literary pursuits, and can produce many testimonials as to his ability as a writer, and the general integrity of his character. He would hold in utter disdain the meanness of copying and employing as his own the ideas and modes of expression of any author, living or dead. He is employed by the defendants as a writer, at a considerable salary. He is the author of the *Christmas Ghost Story*. From the *Christmas Carol* and Mr. Lee's notes and memoranda thereon (which pointed out certain beauties and many defects) the deponent, in accordance with his custom for many years past, proceeded to analyse the book, for the purpose of reoriginating the tale or plot thereof in an abridged and synoptical form. Besides the defects, or want of harmony, pointed out by Mr. Lee, the deponent detected so many others as to induce him in numerous instances to abandon the plot, and substitute what he verily believes to be a more artistical style of expression and of incident. Though the deponent, had he been so disposed, could have cut the book into fragments, and then effected a flimsy reunion by tacking such fragments together with a few thread-like sentences, as is the custom in many periodical works, such would have been mutilation rather than abridgment or reorigination. The deponent has, at times, analytically re-originated several of Dickens's works, including *The Old Curiosity Shop* and *Barnaby Rudge*. The inscribed volume in Mr. Lee's affidavit referred to was taken to Dickens's residence by the deponent's son, William Hewitt, who is not at present in London. The deponent verily believes that Dickens has, however unconsciously, been indebted to the critical remarks made by the deponent from time to time in *Parley's Library*, for the germ of more than one of his productions, and also verily believes Dickens to be more indebted to Washington Irving for the materials of his *Christmas Carol* than the deponent is to Dickens as regards the *Christmas Ghost Story*. The deponent's avowed purpose in his analytical abridgments, as exemplified in an extract from his address on the commencement of *Parley's Library*, is to afford to the youth of both sexes such an introduction to illustrious writers as will engender fierce and irrepressible desire to become more intimately acquainted with the productions of these master spirits, with the result that they will be allured to exercise their own powers in producing for themselves an analysis of every book worthy of recollection. The deponent verily believes that the humbler classes have neither time nor money to expend upon larger, or high-priced works. The conveyance of faithful pictures in miniature of expensive works is, and for many years has been, the deponent's study and practice. In dealing with any author's work, he has always candidly laid bare its quality; and on the present occasion he in the honest exercise of his judgment, has in numerous particulars wholly abandoned the plot of the *Christmas Carol*, in order to improve the tale and render the same the more consistent, and to give greater effect to the leading incidents therein. He verily believes for the reason hereinbefore adduced, and many others which he is ready to substantiate, that the *Christmas Carol* is not only not colourably imitated in the *Christmas Ghost Story*, but that there has been an entire abandonment of Dickens's work in all that can be deemed its essentials.

George Stiff, of 16 *Gloucester Place, Camden Town, in the County of Middlesex, says:*

For many years past he has been an artist, draughtsman, and engraver. Before the 1st of January he, from Mr. Hewitt's manuscript, designed, engraved, and invented three illustrations to the *Christmas Ghost Story*, and these illustrations have been reproduced in the two parts of the story. He has never read the *Christmas Carol*, nor did he ever in any way or manner examine the plates. Since the granting of the present injunction, he has carefully compared these plates with his illustrations, and verily believes that there is no figure, character, scene, or personage in the *Christmas Carol* at all resembling any figure, character, scene, or personage in his pictures. He received a considerable sum of money for his three inventions, and he believes the defendants to be wholly incapable of knowingly infringing the copyright or property of any author whatever, inasmuch as he has frequently heard them express their decided disapprobation of the practice, or system, of wholesale verbatim extract, with short connecting paragraphs, prevailing in many literary journals. He believes from his experience that re-written abridgments and productions of popular works, such as those published by the defendants, are not only beneficial to the public, but by enhancing the popularity of the original author, contribute in many ways to such author's pecuniary benefit, as was the case with *Masterman Ready* and *The Last of the Barons*, and in numerous other instances. The deponent further believes that by the abridged reproduction of the *Christmas Carol* in the candid manner set forth in the title of the *Christmas Ghost Story*, a positive benefit, instead of injury as charged, would be conferred on Dickens's copyright and reputation.

Having thus, by the exercise of much skill, talent, and invention, reoriginated in brief the affidavits of the publisher, author, and artist responsible for the piracy, I will venture to make a few comments upon their statements before dealing with the testimony of the two literary experts.

Lee, it will be observed, devotes much space to an attempt to saddle Dickens with express notice of earlier piracies, and Hewitt confirms all that he says, and alleges that the volume containing these piracies was actually left at Dickens's house by Hewitt junior. There is, however, no affidavit of the messenger, he unfortunately being out of London just then. All this shows how much the defendants relied upon laches and acquiescence in respect of former piracies as an answer to the plaintiff's action as regards the *Carol*. To my mind the whole story of the inscribed copy is intrinsically improbable, and I decline to accept it on the oaths of such deponents as Lee and Hewitt.

Lee's affidavit is illuminating evidence of the wholesale

manner in which the works of popular writers were "reoriginated" seventy years ago. The mere string of names which he gives proves this; and one may fairly assume that Messrs. Lee and Haddock were not alone in the field. The statement of Lee that over seventy thousand copies of one number of the *Library* had been printed, though startling, is probably true; and as hereafter appears, one of the literary deponents speaks of a sale of more than fifty thousand copies of *The Old Curiosity Shop* piracy. The profits of such circulations as these must, like Hewitt's salary, have been "considerable."

The allegations that some of Dickens's books had not been deemed worthy of reorigination, and that he had been indebted to the *Library* for "germs" and suggestions are masterpieces of impertinence, but what amuses me most is Lee's assumption of the editorial dignity. He asserts in stately language that in the exercise of his usual avocations he critically examined the *Carol* as soon as it appeared. The fruits of this examination were communicated to Hewitt in the form of notes and an opinion; the notes according to their recipient being of a severely critical character and relating mostly to the book's defects. This reads rather well, notwithstanding the absence of the documents, or of any evidence accounting for the same, but Lee's signature to his affidavit makes belief impossible. There is a laborious illiteracy about that "Richard Egan Lee" which speaks for itself.

I am afraid that *Parley's Illuminated Library* was a sort of double-barrelled piracy as regards its very name. In *The Times* report of the motions against the four booksellers it appears that Talfourd complained that the title was so printed as to render it doubtful whether or not "that gentleman" was the conductor. The "gentleman" referred to must have been our old friend Samuel Griswold Goodrich, the American whose pen-name was "Peter Parley." So much for the *Parley's!* The *Illuminated* had apparently been lifted from Douglas Jerrold's *Illuminated Magazine*, which had come into existence in 1843.

One of the two literary affidavits came upon me as a surprise, for the deponent was no other than the late E. L. Blanchard, so well known to my generation as a dramatic critic and writer of Drury Lane pantomimes. The other was George Mudie. His name, too, seemed to invite confidence. As his affidavit was filed a day earlier than Blanchard's, I will deal with it first.

George Mudie, of Stanhope Street, Strand, in the County of Middlesex, Gentleman, says :

He has carefully perused the *Christmas Ghost Story.* He was for many years editor of the *Sun* daily newspaper, and has devoted more than thirty years to literary pursuits, and has obtained considerable literary reputation as an author of numerous works in philology and political economy, and as a writer of books of poetry and fiction which have been very extensively circulated. His practice and study for so many years have made him an expert as regards the matters in question. He has compared the *Ghost Story* with the *Carol,* and is of opinion that there is not the slightest ground for denominating the *Ghost Story* a colourable imitation of the *Carol,* inasmuch as although the characters and some of the incidents of the *Ghost Story* are avowedly derived from the *Carol,* as appears on the title of the *Ghost Story,* yet the difference of thought, style, matter, and quality of the two works, many of the best parts of each not being in the other, and the extreme disparity of price between the two could not by any possibility allow of the abridgment being taken, or sold, for the original. But, as the deponent verily believes, so far from the defendants' publication injuring the plaintiff, the deponent has invariably found that the treating of works of the deponent and others in this way has not injured the works so treated, and the deponent believes and declares that the defendants' condensation or abridgment of *The Old Curiosity Shop,* whereof he has been informed by the publishers that more than fifty thousand copies were circulated, was beneficial to the plaintiff. The many years which the deponent has spent in literary engagements have given him a certain knowledge of the nature of public opinion, and from which he is well assured that the readers of the defendants' publication, which is sold at a penny, and those of the *Carol,* which is sold at five shillings, belong to a totally different class; and the deponent is also assured that the buyers of the *Ghost Story* would not have bought the *Carol*, and that the defendants' publication being intended for, and in fact, bought by those whose circumstances prevent them, not only from buying but for the most part from even hiring, a work of higher price, is calculated to add to the plaintiff's popularity, as well as to benefit society.

Edward Leman Blanchard, of 7 Clements Inn, Strand, in the County of Middlesex, Gentleman, says:

He has devoted many years to literary pursuits, and has attained considerable success and profit as a dramatic author and a writer of works of romance and fiction. He has carefully perused the *Christmas Ghost Story*. The deponent's practice and study for so many years have enabled him to judge the matters in question. He has compared the *Carol* with the *Ghost Story*, and is of opinion that there is not the slightest ground for denominating the *Ghost Story* a colourable imitation or piracy of the *Carol*, inasmuch as although the characters and some of the incidents contained in the *Ghost Story* are avowedly derived from the *Carol*, as appears in the title of the *Ghost Story*, yet the difference of style, matter, and quantity of the two works, many of the best parts of each not being in the other, and the extreme disparity of price between the two would effectually prevent the abridgment from being taken, or sold, as the original; but as the deponent believes the *Ghost Story* will materially contribute to the popularity of and consequent demand for the *Carol*, which work, as well as others of the plaintiff's books, are very similar in many parts and passages to Washington Irving's writings. The many years which the deponent has spent in literary engagements have given him a certain knowledge of the nature of public opinion, and from which he is well assured that the readers of the *Ghost Story*, which is sold at a penny, and those of the *Carol*, which is sold at five shillings, belong to a totally different class of society; and the deponent is also assured that the buyers of the *Ghost Story* would not have bought the *Carol*, and that the defendants' publication, being intended for, and in fact bought, by those whose circumstances prevent them not only from purchasing, but for the most part from even hiring, a work of higher price, is calculated to add to the plaintiff's popularity, as well as to benefit society.

I will reserve my comments upon these affidavits until after I have laid before the reader what happened on the hearing of the motion to dissolve the injunction.

Dickens made an affidavit in answer to the defendants' evidence, but this goes only to the allegation of laches and acquiescence. He was, no doubt, advised that, no matter how monstrous the contention that because he had acquiesced in the earlier piracies, he was precluded from stopping the piracy of the *Carol* might seem to a layman, this contention was raisable in a Court of Equity and it must be met.

Charles Dickens says:

He has read the affidavits of Lee and Hewitt. He left England for America on the 4th of January 1842, and was absent until the following June. He denies that before Christmas 1841, or at any other time, he received the inscribed volume of *Parley's Library*. If he did receive any such book, he never read it, or was made aware of the alleged analysation, abridgment, and reorigination of *The Old Curiosity Shop* and *Barnaby Rudge*, or either of them. In February 1842, the deponent being then at a public entertainment in the city of Boston, a printed copy, purporting to have been published in England, or an unauthorised version of *The Old Curiosity Shop* was shown to him by Dr. Palfrey of Boston, but the deponent looked but cursorily at the same, and did not then, or at any other time, read it, nor had he any notice or knowledge of the nature or contents thereof, save from the same having been shown to him as aforesaid, and from his having cursorily looked at it. The deponent does not know whether such printed copy was a copy of the said volume or any part thereof, but save as aforesaid he, to the best of his recollection and belief, denies that he has at any time seen, or read, any copy of the said volume, or any part thereof. And the deponent says that he has never sanctioned, or knowingly permitted, anyone to copy or imitate the *Carol*, *The Old Curiosity Shop*, or *Barnaby Rudge*, or any of them, but that as soon as he knew of the *Carol* infringement he took the present proceedings to prevent the same.

The references in this affidavit to Dickens's visit to America are not without interest. It is impossible to identify the public entertainment at which Dr. Palfrey showed him a piratical version of *The Old Curiosity Shop*, for his stay in Boston was nothing less than a series of public entertainments. The following sentences, extracted from a letter which he wrote to Mitton on the 31st of January 1842, ten days after his arrival there, speak for themselves:

> I can give you no conception of my welcome here. There never was a king or emperor on the earth so cheered and followed by crowds, and entertained in public at splendid balls and dinners, and waited on by public bodies and deputations of all kinds. . . . You cannot imagine what it is. I have five great public dinners on hand at this moment, and invitations from every town and village and city in the States.

Lee and Haddock's motion to dissolve the injunction came on before Knight Bruce at Westminster on the 18th January 1844. The counsel briefed for the moving parties were Thomas Oliver Anderdon, Q.C., and C. J. Shebbeare. Anderdon was a bencher of Lincoln's Inn, and a barrister of twenty years' standing; Shebbeare was a mere forensic infant, called at Gray's Inn in November 1837. I have no doubt that they were both persons of the highest respectability, but I know nothing of their careers.

Anderdon and his junior each had a full innings, and we may be sure that Shebbeare began a pretty copious address by expressing a modest fear that he could not profitably add anything to what had fallen from his leader. When both the learned gentlemen had run down, Knight Bruce—to the disappointment of Talfourd, who had sat up until three that morning to prepare his speech—gave judgment dismissing the motion. If, he said, the defendants chose to force the plaintiff to submit his case to a jury, this course was open to them; but they must say yea or nay within a week, and the injunction must be continued pending the trial of the common law action. *The Times* report of the hearing will be found in the Appendix.

Luckily Forster was not present, and thus we have Dickens's own account, contained in a letter written to his friend the same day:

> The pirates are beaten flat. . . . They are bruised, bloody, battered, smashed, squelched, and utterly undone. Knight Bruce would not hear Talfourd, but instantly gave judgment. He had interrupted Anderton (*sic*) constantly by asking him to produce a passage which was not an expanded or contracted idea from my book. And at every successive passage he cried out: "That is Mr. Dickens's case. Find another!" He said that there was not a shadow of doubt upon the matter. That there was no authority which could bear a construction in their favour; the piracy going beyond all previous instances. They might mention it again in a week, he said, if they liked, and might have an issue if they pleased, but they would probably consider it unnecessary after that strong expression of his opinion. Of course I will stand by what we have agreed as to the only terms of compromise with the printers. I am determined that I will have an apology for their affidavits. The other men may pay their costs and get out of it, but I will stick to my friend the author.

Dickens's advisers did well when, in exercise of the right which a plaintiff then enjoyed, they assigned the causes to Knight Bruce. There is an excellent sketch of this vice-chancellor in Mr. Registrar Manson's *Builders of our Law under Queen Victoria*, from which we learn that he was a humorist and a master of sarcasm, as well as a loather of technicalities, and a very learned judge. One of his epigrams, which Mr. Manson quotes, gives a taste of his quality—

> The curate's eyes our ladies praise:
> I never see their light divine;
> He always shuts them when he prays,
> And when he preaches closes mine.

I think there must have been a momentary closing of one of his Honour's eyes when he offered the defendants a trial at common law. The defendants' evidence had been read at the bar, and to him its falsity must have been apparent. Possibly he figured to himself the appearance of the deponents in the witness-box, with Talfourd cross-examining!

Such of my readers as shall have the curiosity to read *The Times* report will see that both Anderdon and his junior made much of the defence of laches and acquiescence. This no doubt was their only chance, but when in his address Anderdon complained of the plaintiff having sued in chancery, he must have spoken with his tongue in his cheek. At common law this defence could not have been raised: the defendants might have pleaded estoppel, but that would have been quite another thing.

The only authorities referred to in *The Times* report are *Dodsley* v. *Kinnersley* (1 Ambler, Case 212), and *Wilkins* v. *Aikin* (18 Vesey 422). The first of these is a judgment of Sir Thomas Clarke, Master of the Rolls, given in 1761. The Dodsleys, as assignees of Johnson, sought to restrain the publication of the *Grand Magazine of Magazines*, containing an abridgment of *Rasselas.* They failed, on the ground that the reprint was a fair abridgment, and as such, not a piracy. The report shows that not above one-tenth of the original work had been reprinted. *Wilkins* v. *Aikin* was decided by Lord Eldon in 1810. In that case piracy was alleged in respect of an illustrated essay on Grecian Antiquities. Eldon thought that the plaintiff's rights had been prejudiced, but he dissolved the interim injunction restraining publication, and only put the defendant under terms to keep an account pending the verdict of a jury. Technically speaking, this was in those days a maintenance of the injunction. Eldon's words were: "where there is a fair question, the injunction ought not to be dissolved . . . but, maintaining the injunction, an action should be brought forthwith. The proper course in this instance will be to permit this work to be sold in the meantime: the defendant undertaking to account according to the result of the action." This has an odd sound to a modern ear, but I learned, more years ago than I care to remember, that there is no questioning Lord Eldon's terminology. It happened thuswise: the present Lord Chancellor, then a new "silk," was addressing Mr. Justice Kay—"*But how do you get over so-and-so?*" asked the judge, quoting a passage from the judgment under discussion. Mr. Haldane, with exquisite blandness, suggested that it was merely a "loose expression." Kay threw up his hands. *A loose expression?—and in Lord Eldon's mouth!*

Knight Bruce, in his judgment in *Dickens* v. *Lee* as reported in *The Times*, set out the principle on which, according to Eldon, a question of piracy, or no piracy, must be dealt with. The application of this principle to *Dickens* v. *Lee* left the defendants without a leg to stand on. Their counsel must have known what the law was when they went into court: hence the insistence upon the defence of laches and acquiescence.

Mr. Registrar Hussey's note adds a scrap of information to what we learn from *The Times*. In the margin of his book is the following memorandum—"Lewis *v.* Fullerton in Beavan, quoted by Mr. Anderdon as to 'imitating' Mr. Dickens's work." It is difficult to believe that *Lewis* v. *Fullarton* (2 Beavan, 6), can have done the defendants any good, for the judgment was to the effect that if in any work the author mixed up another's literary matter with his own, he must be restrained from publishing the part that was not his; and if this meant that such injunction prevented the publication of the rest, he had only himself to blame. This case had been decided by Lord Langdale in 1839. The fact that Bacon had been one of the defendant's counsel may have been the cause of his employment in *Dickens* v. *Lee.*

Though in a letter to Forster, written two days after the motion, Dickens spoke of "the agony of Talfourd at Knight

Bruce's not hearing him," I think we may be sure that this feeling wore off during the delivery of the judgment, and that at the close the serjeant was quite ready to rejoice with his client. Now in his fifty-fifth year, Talfourd had made a mark in the House of Commons, and he was something of a personage both in literature and the law. But success had not hardened his heart; and the man who had been intimate with Lamb, Coleridge, Hazlitt and Godwin, and to whom Lytton had dedicated the *Lady of Lyons*, must have had too sympathetic a nature to nurse his own chagrin in the presence of a friend's triumph. And he was something more than Dickens's friend and counsel. The author of *Ion*, and a reformer of the law of copyright, must have felt a keen personal satisfaction that the common enemy had been squelched and utterly undone.

It adds a new interest to Westminster Hall when one thinks of the radiant party which turned out of Knight Bruce's court after judgment had been delivered: Dickens—the eager, beautiful young Dickens of Maclise's drawings—all aglow with his victory, and bubbling over with thanks to Talfourd and the rest; even Bacon, perhaps a little flushed, and Mitton nearly as excited as the plaintiff himself; Bach somewhere in the rear, I fancy, carrying a bag, and fully conscious that his affidavit had contributed to the grand result. It was some years later that—in England, at all events—Dickens ventured upon a beard, or moustache. Possibly all the members of that triumphant group were clean-shaved. But as regards Bacon I do not feel sure: my recollection of the old vice-chancellor is associated with whiskers of a wild and miscellaneous character. So far as I can ascertain, all lawyers' wigs were powdered seventy years ago, and the practice died out gradually as the generation passed away. Bacon's wig was powdered to the last.

Westminster Hall has another association with Dickens in his happiest mood. Some ten years before the *Carol* litigation he had made his first appearance as an author. The piece was a story called *A Dinner at Poplar Walk*, and it was afterwards included in the *Sketches by Boz*, under the name of *Mr. Minns and his Cousin.* Stealthily one evening at twilight he had dropped the manuscript into the letter-box of the *Old Monthly Magazine*, up a dark court in Fleet Street. It was in the Strand that he bought the number containing his sketch. "On which occasion," he says, "I walked down to Westminster Hall and turned into it for half an hour, because my eyes were so dimmed with joy and pride, that they could not bear the street and were not fit to be seen there." In the fainter light he could pace up and down and weave his day-dreams, without anybody noticing those wet eyes. We all see visions at one-and-twenty, and the future laughs them to scorn. But it gave Dickens even more than he dreamed of; the rosiest fancies of that half-hour were but a pale shadow of the reality to come.

I have already digressed so often and so shamelessly that, grown hardened in iniquity, I will, while we are still in Westminster Hall, say a word about the marvellous faithfulness of Dickens's sketches of lawyers and their clerks. His mind during the two years of his clerkships must have been like a photographic plate, or to put it more poetically, "wax to receive and marble to retain." Only those who, like the present writer, have grown grey in the profession, can fully appreciate the extent and accuracy of his knowledge. Things are very different now, but forty years ago there was much left of the legal world which those wonderful young eyes had studied when George the Fourth was king. And the men who were old when I was young had stories to tell of those earlier days. I recollect one ancient, a managing common-law clerk, who could remember the green numbers of *Pickwick* coming out month by month, and who had many anecdotes of spunging-houses and other vanished things mentioned therein.

This veteran was a worthy and responsible type of his day and generation, but even he had more than a touch of kinship with the Georgian law clerks whom Dickens knew. For example, he was a dungeon of learning as regards the practice, but he could never be prevailed upon to initiate a neophyte into its mysteries. Any appeal on the part of a would-be disciple to share his toil at Judges' Chambers, then situate in the Rolls Garden, and vulgarly known as the "Bear-garden," was diplomatically put aside; the fact being that though my friend and his brother managing-clerks were religiously absent from their employers' offices for some five hours every day, very little of this time was spent under the shadow of the Record Office. There was no occasion for these patriarchs to waste their energies upon squabbles before judges or masters; they of their ripe experience knew what orders the facts justified, and with a little give and take on both sides, the small blue oblong summonses of those days could be adorned with "consent endorsements," quite as effectual as those of the judicial officers themselves. This excellent arrangement left ample time for social conversation and reasonable conviviality. I have been told—but I do not vouch for the fact—that the Rising Sun in Wych Street was the meeting-place of the club—for such in fact it was—at which these choice spirits agreed upon their orders, and enjoyed the leisure to which they were so justly entitled. Other times: other manners! None of the legal business of to-day is transacted in public-houses, and the Dickens type of law clerk is extinct.

Another instance of the receptivity of that youthful brain occurs to me as I write. I feel sure that the Wilkins Flasher episode in *Pickwick* was a reminiscence of Dickens's boyhood. Imagination enters into the sketch hardly at all, but as a photograph it is wonderful. What lover of *Pickwick* can make a sale, or transfer, at the Bank, without remembering Wilkins Flasher, Esquire, and his friend Simmery? My belief is that we owe these portraits to the fact that in 1827, or 1828, Blackmore sent his junior clerk to the City, as escort to some small client who had to sell out stock; and the broker and a friend kept the two waiting, and talked before them as freely as if they had been the chairs in which they sat. Great creatures of the Flasher type were conscious of their own importance; they could bet and gossip regardless of the office boy in his first surtout and his equally obscure companion. But they would not play such pranks as these before an older Dickens: therefore, if the sketch be a photograph, it must be dated back to those early years. Every detail of the experience stamped itself upon that marvellous brain, and nearly ten years later, when *Pickwick* was nearing the end, Dickens could mint-off the impression in all its freshness.

At two- or three-and-thirty he was still a boy in one respect—the occupation of the moment filled his whole mind. When in 1845 he was getting up a performance of *Every Man in His Humour*, he so threw himself into his part that for the time being he wrote and talked like Bobadil. Even the language of the *Carol* affidavits made an impression on him which lasted for at least five weeks. On the 26th of February 1844 he went down to Liverpool, having Bacon with him as far as Watford, "and very pleasant." At Liverpool he delivered an address at the Mechanics' Institution, and he sent home a glowing account of his triumph, written in hot haste just after the meeting. He threw this into the form of an affidavit, beginning with his name, address, and description, and containing as many "Thats" and "saiths" as are peppered about the evidence epitomised above. We who practise the law nowadays ought to be thankful that affidavits are no longer couched in the third person, and that if he will, a draftsman may state his facts to the Court as simply as if he were writing to a friend.

The group in Westminster Hall that morning in 1844 must have soon melted away. Bacon would have work to do in court, or at 10 New Square, and Talfourd would be wanted in the Common Pleas. The serjeants were busy in 1844. Ten years earlier, Brougham had purported to abolish by royal mandate their exclusive right to audience before the Common Pleas *in banc*, but in 1839 the Court had felt justified in treating the mandate as a nullity; and now the gentlemen with the black lozenges on their wigs were enjoying their own again. But not for long! The monopoly came to an end in the next Trinity Vacation but two. On the 18th of August 1846 the Act to extend to all barristers practising in the superior courts at Westminster the privileges of serjeants-at-law in the Court of Common Pleas received the royal assent.[1] Talfourd was made a judge three years later, and in 1854 he died suddenly of apoplexy, while charging the grand jury at Stafford. Sir Charles Darling has told in hexameters the story of that last assize. Dickens, as all the world knows, died on the 9th of June 1870. Mitton, his friend from boyhood, died in or about 1878.[2] Bacon's long pilgrimage endured till 1895.

I think Dickens must have been a somewhat animated litigant while the motion was in progress. He was not the man to sit still and let Mitton deal with counsel. The long-haired, bright-faced gentleman must have had many a colloquy with Talfourd while Anderdon and Shebbeare were addressing the court—hasty whisperings across the bar: a sore trial to the serjeant, who knew everything that his client could tell him, and who wanted to keep his whole attention on the enemy.

From the fact that Forster made no reference to the motion having come before the court a second time, I assumed that the defendants did not avail themselves of their liberty to mention it again in a week; and if Mr. Pochin had not drawn my attention to the *Jurist*, by which it appeared that the motion was men-

[1] The best account known to me of the royal mandate and its failure is in J. B. Atlay's *Victorian Chancellors* (1906), vol. i. pp. 433–6, a book which is not so widely read as it deserves to be. The scope of the author's researches is amazing, but notwithstanding the mass of information which he has accumulated, his work is as readable as the *Lives of the Chancellors*, while in fairness, accuracy, and literary polish he leaves Campbell far behind.

[2] I assume this from the fact that he does not appear in the *Law List* after that year.

tioned on the 25th of January, I should have remained in ignorance of that day's proceedings. From *The Times* report, printed in the Appendix hereto, it will be seen that on this further hearing Anderdon rejected an olive branch which counsel offered on Dickens's behalf, and stood out for his clients' strict rights, with the result that Dickens was put under terms to bring a common-law action within ten days. But Lee and Haddock did not ride the high horse for long. Forster tells us, as hereinafter appears, that they agreed to apologise and pay costs, and whether this happened before or after the ten days had run out is a matter of no interest to anybody.

The *Jurist* report (8 Jurist, part 1, p. 183) covers both hearings, but it is so technical that in mercy to the general reader I do not reprint it. This report is cited in all the current text-books on copyright; and in running my eye down the table contained in one of them, I came upon a case of *Bradbury* v. *Dickens*, 27 Beaven, 53. The report showed that in 1859 Dickens had made a second appearance in Chancery. This time, however, he was a defendant. The proceedings arose out of his quarrel with Bradbury & Evans, and the consequent discontinuance of *Household Words.* Forster's reference to the litigation is studiously brief, and one can see that he had reasons for not going into the details. But now that nearly forty years have gone by since he wrote, these reasons must have lost their cogency, and there can be no harm in setting out the facts. To the best of my knowledge they have never been extracted from the learned obscurity of Beavan. The report is somewhat long, but the epitome set forth in the Appendix contains the gist of the story.

I have not seen the volume of *Parley's Library* containing the reoriginations of *The Old Curiosity Shop* and *Barnaby Rudge*, nor have I seen No. 16 of *Parley's Illuminated Library* containing the first half of the *Ghost Story*. Probably both are great rarities. The British Museum has no copy of either, and I know of none in private hands. So far as the literary matter of No. 16 is concerned, I would take very little trouble to find the thing, but I should like to see the pictures, in order to compare Stiff's work with the *Carol* plates. On the evidence of both sides, coupled with what fell from Knight Bruce, no reasonable person can feel any doubt that the *Ghost Story* was in all essentials a copy of the *Carol*, and I cannot imagine anyone caring to read Hewitt's "reorigination" for the pleasure of it.

But though I have no longing to study his text, I am sorry that I cannot enrich my own with a few extracts from "the carol or song of sixty lines . . . admirably adapted to the occasion and replete with pathos and poetry." This is a rather long composition according to modern notions, but it was nothing out of the way seventy years ago. Nor need we deduce from this that the nation's lungs are weaker than they used to be. We degenerates rarely drink when we sing, whereas our stout grandsires stayed themselves with flagons. Hewitt's song is a mere snatch as compared with one which I used to hear in my volunteering days. This ballad—popularly supposed to comprise a hundred verses—formed part of the *répertoire* of a veteran sergeant upon our staff. It was called *Hurrah for the Red, White, and Blue!* I was never privileged to hear all of it; for it was our practice, as soon as it had run for about a quarter of its reputed length, to lop off the remainder by the simple expedient of removing the singer's glass.

Although I am unable to put the *Ghost Story* in evidence, so to speak, I feel justified in stigmatising the defendants' case as reeking with perjury; and all things considered, I am not at all sure that the affidavits of the two literary men are not more blameworthy than the rest. After the battle was over Dickens took a philosophical view of these monstrosities—"The further affidavits put in by way of extenuation by the printing rascals *are* rather strong, and give one a pretty correct idea of what the men must be who hold on to the heels of literature," he wrote to Forster on the 20th of January; and later on in the letter is the following passage: "I once thought of printing the affidavits without a word of comment, and sewing them up with *Chuzzlewit.*"

There is one small point in favour of Mudie and Blanchard—neither of them called the piracy a reorigination or an analysis. This seems to show that there was a limit beyond which their consciences would not stretch. But each of them swore that there was not the slightest ground for denominating the *Ghost Story* a colourable imitation, or piracy, of the *Carol.* This was untrue; and to my mind the setting forth of the grounds on which this opinion purported to be based made the lie none the whiter. The suggestion, conveyed by a parenthesis, that the *Carol* and the *Ghost Story* were much on the same level—each full of good things peculiar to itself—is nearly as bad, but it is slipped in so ingeniously that a legal person—the present writer, at all events! —can only laugh at it.

I am unable to give any particulars of George Mudie's life. The "Stanhope Street, Strand" of his affidavit was Stanhope Street, Clare Market, a squalid retreat for a man of letters: even worse than White Lion Street, Islington! All that the British Museum catalogue discloses of his philosophy, political economy, poetry, and fiction is a thin duodecimo and a shilling pamphlet. Each of these bears on the title page a reference to his former editorship of the *Sun.* An extract from the duodecimo's title will sufficiently indicate the nature of the book: *The Grammar of the English language made easy and amusing. . . . For the use of Schools . . . and of Adults whose knowledge of Grammar may be defective.* The pamphlet—issued in 1849—is on the organisation of labour, and as to part, it is an answer to Lamartine's *Trois Mois au Pouvoir.* It is prefaced by a letter addressed to Louis Napoleon, the then President of the French Republic. It will be remembered that the author of these journeyman productions insinuated in his affidavit that he, too, had been "reoriginated," and like Dickens, had benefited by the process. This was a master-stroke!

There is in the Museum catalogue a third publication under the name "George Mudie"; a trumpery pamphlet on the dissolution of an Edinburgh debating society; but as this came out in 1812, I do not think that it can have been written by our deponent. The *Dictionary of National Biography* knows him not. Possibly he was the son of Robert Mudie, "miscellaneous writer," therein named, who near the end of his life did hack work for a Winchester bookseller, and who died at Pentonville in 1842, "leaving the widow of a second marriage in destitution, one son and four daughters." As George had been editor of the *Sun*, I dare say it would not be difficult to trace out particulars of his career, and learn what brought him to a lodging in Clare Market, and an association with Lee and Haddock. But why disturb his ashes? He has probably been dead for half a century, and not a soul remembers his name.

But with E. L. Blanchard the case is different. Five-and-twenty years ago he was one of the best known figures in London, and he went to his grave mourned and respected by all who knew him. The reason why he came forward in support of Lee and Haddock is not far to seek—at that time, he, like Hewitt, was a pillager of other men's brains, and Lee was one of his employers. The business was a shabby one, but we must not blame him overmuch on that score. He was poor, and the trade had gone on for so long without interference that it was almost recognised as lawful. The best of good men, even when they are well off, are none too apt to question the righteousness of anything that brings grist to the mill, provided no disgrace attaches to it. And as regards his affidavit, the mere fact that he had stooped to shabby work is some excuse for the much more serious offence of swearing to the thing that was not. Shakespeare knew how much a man's mind is coloured by his trade:

. . . subdued
To what it works in, like the dyer's hand.

Blanchard, too, was out in defence of his bread and butter. That would incline him to swear up to the mark, without weighing his words very nicely. Few of us—even the lawyers—are creatures of pure reason when the pocket is in question, and Lee's hack could ill afford to have any source of livelihood cut off. The wolf was always near the door. At fifteen the death of his father had brought his schooling to an end, and had thrown him upon his own resources. How for the next few years he kept body and soul together is a mystery. Before he was twenty he had produced thirty dramas, farces, and burlesques, and a number of pantomimes; but in those days the pay of minor dramatists was contemptible, and the probability is that all his labour did not bring him in a hundred pounds. His earnings, even in brighter times, were small. At three-and-thirty his income was less than two hundred a year, and at fifty it was under four, though by then he had made a name, and his pen was always busy.

Years ago, at the seaside, I came upon his *Life and Reminiscences* in a circulating library. The book is much too long for its subject; but I skimmed through it one evening, and it left behind the recollection of a good man whose life had been a hard one patiently borne, and whose small earnings had been largely spent on others. I also remembered that there had been a pretty love story, crowned at last by a marriage which had brightened his latter years. After my search at the Record Office I looked through the book again. It was pleasant to find evidence that Dickens had cherished no rancour against the deponent of 1844. Twenty years later, the *Diary* casually mentions that Blanchard met Dickens near Gad's Hill, and that mutual recognitions were exchanged. I am inclined to think that Blanchard had long forgotten all about the *Carol* litigation, for under date of the 15th of April 1858, his diary contains the following entry: "At night to St. Martin's Hall; hear Dickens read *Christmas Carol*, and delighted." It was his custom to note up any association with the past which a new entry suggested, and he would probably have done so on this occasion if he had remembered *Dickens* v. *Lee*. Dickens may also have forgotten Blanchard's affidavit. But I doubt it; he must have learned in 1844 that the deponent was the son of Blanchard the comedian, and this would have made upon his mind an impression never to be erased.

Unfortunately Blanchard's diary does not begin until June 1844; but though it throws no direct light upon *Dickens* v. *Lee*, there are entries which, coupled with the editorial narrative and footnotes, add not a little to the information which we have about the *Carol* pirates. We learn, for instance, something about the defendant Cleave. A note to page 30 tells us that this man became notorious for his contests with the Government in respect of the floating of unstamped news-sheets. One of these rags was called the *Gazette of Varieties*. Blanchard was a contributor to it, and he did other jobs for the proprietor. On the 5th of March 1846 he records in his diary that he was "at home all day compiling a *Book of Jests* for Cleave." The editorial part of the *Diary and Reminiscences* states that he thought highly of this employer, but never found him flush of money. Mudie was another of Cleave's authors; the philological duodecimo above referred to bears his imprint.

A further note to page 30 states that Stiff was proprietor of the *London Journal*. As only the surname is given, one cannot be sure that he was the deponent who illustrated the *Ghost Story*, and who had frequently heard Messrs. Lee and Haddock express their "decided disapprobation" of certain shady practices in literature. A Mr. Haddock is also referred to, but in this case the name is so uncommon that I think we may safely identify the gentleman with Lee's partner. It is highly improbable that two Haddocks were then swimming in the strange waters which

Blanchard knew. Owing to some editorial oversight, we are told on page 10 that Blanchard in 1844 started a publication called *The Astrologer and Oracle of Destiny*, and we are told on page 29 that the periodical was started by Haddock. From what follows, however, it seems clear that Haddock was the proprietor, and that Blanchard did all the work. Haddock's disappearance from the scene of his labours was so sudden and mysterious that it raised a doubt—not apparently shared by Blanchard—whether he had not been snatched away by the Evil One. Strange to say, the disinclination to fork out, which was a characteristic of Cleave's, was also noticeable in the proprietor of the *Astrologer*.

But of all the editorial footnotes, the most interesting for present purposes is one which refers to *Parley's Library*. The mention of this periodical is merely casual, for the editors knew nothing of the *Carol* litigation. They state in the text that Blanchard wrote a good deal for the *Library*, and a footnote gives some interesting details concerning it. We are told that it was " a popular penny ' mag,' famous for E. L. B.'s potting down of three-volume novels, to wit *Eugene Aram*, *Last Days of Pompeii*, and *Last of the Barons* " ; that the price was threepence for three numbers, and that Blanchard " used to get about ten shillings for potting down these famous works."

We are even fortunate enough to find a mention of Hewitt. The footnote says that he " potted down " *The Old Curiosity Shop* and *Barnaby Rudge* for *Parley's Library*, and describes him as a Manchester sub-editor. Having regard to his salaried connection with Lee and Haddock, and to the fact that he lived in White Lion Street, Islington, his sub-editorship must then have been a thing of the past, but I think we may treat the footnote as accurate, except on this small point, and may assume—though no authority is cited—that it was founded upon some memorandum made by Blanchard. When Hewitt in his affidavit described himself as " editor," he was, no doubt, referring to his coadjutor-editorship with Lee.

Having thus by a very odd chance ascertained that Lee and Haddock paid Blanchard ten shillings for the "reorigination" of a three-volume novel, I think it improbable that the "considerable salary" which they paid to Hewitt exceeded a pound a week. This calculation ignores in their favour the fact that a wage-earner always gets less per job than a piece-worker, and is based upon the assumption that a piratical version of, say, *Eugene Aram*, abridged to fit the dimensions of three numbers of *Parley's Library*, could not be turned out in less than three days. The mere writing would take up most of that time. Seeing that a three-volume novel cost at least a guinea, trade price, and could be hired for sixpence, I think it improbable that Hewitt and his tribe were allowed to work upon, and cut up, printed copies of the books which they "reoriginated." In this connection, it is worth recalling that Lee, Hewitt, and Stiff all swore that Hewitt turned out a manuscript of the *Ghost Story*. Their oaths may not go for much, but the alteration of "Fezziwig" to "Fuzziwig" is, perhaps, a scrap of corroboration—can this have been anything but a slip of the copyist's flying pen, or his misreading of the original? And apart from any evidence, is it intrinsically probable that with books so dear and flesh and blood so cheap, the printers would buy the works which their slaves "potted down"?

Hewitt swears to having been engaged in literary pursuits for thirty-five years. Very likely this statement was true, both as regards the period and the nature of his experience; and remembering how Blanchard was paid for work like his, what a horrible glimpse it gives us into the lives of hack-writers seventy years ago! The mere thought of any literary man working at a salary for a printer whose trade was piracy makes one shudder, and recall the awful days of Grub Street, and the grim legend that Kit Smart and a brother hack leased themselves to a printer for ninety-nine years.

Blanchard spent his youth in that strange under-world, but

he was never a salaried hack, tied to one employer, and he had the future to look forward to. Hewitt, however, must have been an elderly man in 1844, and the probabilities are that his pound a week—or whatever the amount may have been—was all that stood between him and the workhouse. If in his earlier days he had sub-edited a newspaper, he must have come down in the world. It would be easy to draw inferences and moralise upon the result, but in so doing there would be no profit. Let us pass on with a hope that his son William, who made the alleged journey to Dickens's house, was not brought up to his father's trade ; and in charity to the poor drudge, let us remember that seventy years ago there were lower depths of hack authorship than those in which he laboured! Penny weeklies of what may be called the "Holywell-street" type were common then, but I have come across nothing to suggest that Lee and Haddock had any connection with this industry. The manufacture of these "obscene publications" continued until Lord Campbell brought it to an end.

Before I bid good-bye to the literary under-world of Hewitt's time, let me say that I have had the curiosity to make a pilgrimage to White Lion Street, Islington, in search of his abode. The *Directory* for 1844 shows that the then occupant of No. 101 was Mrs. Sophia Offord, grocer, who no doubt had him as a lodger. White Lion Street is a long dreary byway, running out of High Street, Islington, a few paces north of the Angel, and ending at Penton Street. No. 101 is no longer in existence. The site of eight, or nine, little houses, including Mrs. Offord's, is now covered by an optician's manufactory. The grocer's shop of 1844 stood on the north side of the street, a few doors from the Islington end, and nearly opposite the White Lion public-house. My companion on the excursion—an American gentleman whose worship of Dickens made him uncharitable towards the pirates—drew my attention to this establishment, and ventured upon a surmise that when Hewitt died, a falling off of the takings had been observable. My friend's rough estimate of the amount was a pound a week.

Some five years after Dickens filed his bills against the *Carol* pirates, the defendant Strange was taken into Chancery by an "orator" of such exalted station that the obscure printer became one of the notorieties of his age. Even now, Strange's audacious attempt to make money out of stolen royal etchings is not quite forgotten.

This man, or—to quote the unkind language of Prince Albert's affidavit—"his confederate or confederates," had obtained possession of sixty-three etchings, the work of Queen Victoria and her Consort, the same "being principally of subjects of private and domestic interest to themselves," and his intention was to publicly exhibit the stolen goods. Of the various reports of *Prince Albert* v. *Strange* which are in existence, I have consulted that beginning on page 25 of the first volume of Macnaghten and Gordon. Strange seems to have admitted as soon as the cause was launched that he was not entitled to hold a show of the etchings, but he fought hard for the right to circulate particulars of them in the form of a sixpenny catalogue printed by himself. Knight Bruce stopped him by injunction, and Lord Cottenham, before whom the case came on appeal, upheld the vice-chancellor. Strange was directed to pay the costs of the rehearing, but whether Prince Albert received any benefit from this direction I do not know.[1]

I have found at the Record Office nothing in any of the *Carol* suits of later date than Blanchard's affidavit, but as my search was not pressed far, it is quite possible that the records may include the order made in *Dickens* v. *Lee* on the 25th January 1844, and

[1] I am indebted to Mr. W. H. Peet, of Messrs. Longmans, for reminding me of *Prince Albert* v. *Strange*, and identifying the defendant with one of Dickens's opponents. Lord Cottenham finally disposed of the matter in February 1849, the bill having been filed in the preceding October. Sir John Romilly (then Solicitor-General), Talfourd, and Mr. (afterwards Lord Justice) James were the Prince's counsel.

a subsequent order in each of the five causes, staying proceedings and directing payment of the plaintiff's costs. These orders, however, would not disclose anything which we do not know already. It appears from Forster that an arrangement was come to whereby Dickens was to receive an ample public apology and payment of the costs, but the *Life* goes on to say that in the end he got nothing.

The amount of his costs of the five causes must have been serious: probably at least as many hundred-pounds. Chancery litigation under the old system was a ruinous business. In *The Times* of the 18th of January 1844 I came upon a paragraph to the effect that the expense of a certain bill and answer was estimated at seven-hundred pounds. These documents were, of course, abnormally bulky, but even Bacon's five little compositions, each containing a bare three-thousand words, must have cost something. During my earlier searches, I wondered why Dickens's advisers had let him go to the expense of proceeding against the four booksellers, as well as against the actual producers of the *Ghost Story*. It seemed extravagant to start litigation on that scale, without first seeing what the effect of an injunction against the printers would be. But later on I found the key of the mystery—it was not until after the five interim injunctions had been obtained that Dickens knew for certain who had produced the *Ghost Story*.

Mitton must have had ten dreadful days between the 8th and the 18th of January seventy years ago, but for a young practitioner the *Carol* job was a little gold mine. My legal readers will understand that, given the proceedings in one of the causes, the creation of the other four sets would be little more than a matter of law-stationery, but notwithstanding this, each cause would carry a separate and complete bill of costs. The mere thought is enough to make a beginner lick his lips! But, however large the amount of the costs, we may be sure that Dickens paid up like a man; and the relations between him and Mitton being so intimate, I dare say the settlement was enlivened by a reference to Mr. Solomon Pell and the job on which he "boarded, lodged, and washed for six months afterwards." Dickens gave his friend the manuscript of the *Christmas Carol*. It would be fantastic to doubt that this gift was a mark of his appreciation of Mitton's services in defence of the copyright. One is sorry to know that the recipient sold it a few years after Dickens's death.

I should be ungrateful if I did not put on record a word of thanks for the courtesy and assistance which I received from the officials of the Record Office. So abundant was their sympathy that they seemed quite grieved at the outlay which my search involved. The men are splendid and the place is a wonder, but may I venture to hint that some accommodation for coats and hats ought to be provided? The weather was nearly always wet when I went to the "Legal Search Room," and it was not pleasant to work, with a moist vestment hanging over one's chair.

The other searchers afforded an interesting study during my intervals of enforced leisure. Particularly the young ladies! Some of these were of the Girton type, and it was pretty to see two curly heads bent over a parchment roll, while one damsel read the crabbed Latin at sight, and the other checked her translation. From a searcher of the ruder sex I gained a curious piece of information. Though the fact that, now and again, he muttered a bad word under his breath as he pored over a very faint script, was clear evidence that he had no connection with the law, I ventured to offer him a word of brotherly sympathy upon the severity of his task. He took this in good part, and assured me that there had been no decent ink since the thirteenth century.

I will now deal with a question which has probably occurred to the reader's mind more than once—was Dickens's game worth the candle? He was of opinion that he got nothing out of the litigation but expense and worry, and we have evidence that his onslaught upon the *Carol* pirates did not secure an immunity from like depredations in the future. Forster writes as follows:

> . . . A couple of years later, upon repetition of the wrong he had suffered in so gross a form that proceedings were again advised by Talfourd and others, he wrote to me from Switzerland the condition of mind to which his experience had brought him. "My feeling about the —— is the feeling common, I suppose, to three-fourths of the community in our happiest of all countries; and that is, that it is better to suffer a great wrong than to have recourse to the much greater wrong of the law. I shall not easily forget the expense, and anxiety, and horrible injustice of the *Carol* case, wherein, in asserting the plainest right on earth, I was really treated as if I were the robber instead of the robbed. Upon the whole, I would certainly much rather NOT proceed.

The reader will remember that before Dickens went into chancery, Talfourd and Forster had "repeatedly urged" him to take proceedings. One is inclined to think that their advice was injudicious. Notwithstanding the injunctions obtained against the *Carol* pirates, the trade continued to flourish; and it is hard to believe that there had ever been a reasonable probability of the plaintiff in that litigation recovering anything from his adversaries—there is an unquotable old proverb which tells what happens to him who sues a beggar. Dickens learned the truth of this, and he declined to be egged-on to a second attack. Forster, by the by, when he was writing the *Life*, did not trouble to verify his recollection of the proceedings of 1844, or he would not have stated that they extended to the *Chuzzlewit* pirates.

But however futile and disappointing the litigation proved to be, I do not believe that it brought Dickens nothing but vexation and money loss, for I am certain that when he came to write *Bleak House*, he found the experience useful; and I am not sure that without it, *Bleak House* would ever have been written. I do not suggest that he got all—or anything like all—of his knowledge of the chancery labyrinth from proceedings which lasted for only three weeks. That would be absurd. Many things went to the making of *Bleak House.* The " man from Shropshire " and his grievances came out of a pamphlet written by Mr. William Challinor, of Leek. I happened to sit next to the author at the Solicitors' Benevolent Association dinner in 1887. He then told me how he came to write this pamphlet and how he had sent it to Dickens, and had corresponded with him about it. He afterwards lent it to me. Even then it was unobtainable, but fortunately the Law Society has a copy. The title is, *The Court of Chancery ; its inherent Defects,* and the date is 1849.

As regards the chancery procedure in open court, Dickens could draw upon his experiences as a reporter. But they were nearly twenty years old when he wrote *Bleak House ;* and it is not putting the case too high to suggest that he may have picked up a hint or two while Knight Bruce, on the 11th of January 1844, was tearing through the thirty-six matters disclosed by the registrar's minute book. This book shows that in one of the cases—nowadays we should call the thing a " further consideration "—at least eleven counsel appeared. This may well have inspired a famous passage in *Bleak House,* which I have often heard lawyers refer to : *Eighteen of Mr. Tangle's learned friends, each armed with a little summary of eighteen hundred sheets, bob up like eighteen hammers in a pianoforte, make eighteen bows, and drop into their eighteen places of obscurity.*

Mr. Birrell in the third of his delightful Lectures on Trusts has given a luminous sketch of the proceedings in old-time administration suits, and has pointed out how futile and extravagant most of the further considerations used to be. There was little, or nothing, to consider, but many learned gentlemen were briefed—with fees of five-and-one—to do no more than bow like Mr. Tangle's friends. This state of things continued down to my time. But whereas in the *Bleak House* days the eighteen learned gentlemen, well assured that everything was for the best in the best of all possible worlds, were only too glad to rise, and thus proclaim the fact of their employment, the moral atmosphere was different forty, or fifty, years later, and counsel briefed on further considerations, preferred to efface themselves, and stick to their seats like limpets. There was a general feeling that the thing was not quite defensible ; possibly there was also a little apprehension that if the judge's attention were drawn to the number of briefs, he might raise unpleasant questions to be determined later on by the taxing-master. An old friend of mine, an equity junior of great experience, waxed eloquent upon this subject whenever one of these superfluous briefs came into his hands. Being a churchwarden, he used to quote Isaiah, and declare that *his* strength was to sit still.

Challinor gave Dickens a specific case of hardship, of which the author of *Bleak House* made good use, but it has never been suggested that his indebtedness extended further than this. It is on record that *The Court of Chancery ; its inherent Defects,* did not come to his notice until after the first number of *Bleak House* had appeared. I may, therefore, eliminate this pamphlet as an element in the question I am now discussing, and I think it may be assumed that Dickens had little, or nothing, to do with chancery while he was at Blackmore's office in Gray's Inn.

Whence, therefore, did he get the knowledge which inspired him with so much hatred ? Not, I think, from his early experience as a reporter in the Lord Chancellor's Court. The most glaring faults of a judicial system are rarely brought before the public eye : it is the dark places of the earth that are full of cruelty. The more august a tribunal, the greater is the inclination of all who practise before it to keep ugly things out of sight. Lyndhurst's court, with the mace and seal in the foreground, and a fringe of liveries and court-suits in the rear, was no fitting theatre for the display of the more repulsive incidents of chancery practice. They would, of course, peep out now and then, but the prevailing atmosphere was one of high courtesy and judicial calm. Lyndhurst himself was irresistible, as we know from the portrait which we have in the third chapter of *Bleak House.* Could any outsider such as Dickens—no matter how imaginative and warm-hearted—fully understand what lay behind the public amenities of the High Court of Chancery ? If not, how could he have been strung-up to the pitch of *Bleak House?* The chronicler of *Jarndyce* v. *Jarndyce* felt the suitors' wrongs as if they were his own : every line relating to the suit pulses with a bitter sense of personal injury. How is this to be accounted for, except by reference to the proceedings of 1844 ?

The letter quoted above proves beyond all dispute that this litigation had left behind a sense of injustice, which was still rankling after the lapse of two years. *Bleak House* was not begun until late in 1851, but when, in the first chapter, the key-note of the book is struck, we find Dickens in the same mood, and giving expression to his feelings in much the same terms : *It is better to suffer a great wrong than to have recourse to the much greater wrong of the law,* says the letter of 1846 ; and here is an extract from the book of nearly six years later : *This is the Court of Chancery . . . there is not an honourable man among its practitioners who would not give—who does not often give—the warning, " Suffer any wrong that can be done you, rather than come here ! "*

I will push this contention no further, and I will wind up my little book with a proposition to which I think all my readers can subscribe—if *Bleak House* was in any way a by-product of the litigation of 1844, Dickens got something in return for what he spent ; and all the countless readers of his book, to say nothing of the men and women who have benefited by the reforms which it helped to bring about, have reason to be thankful that he became Lord Lyndhurst's " orator," and fought the three-weeks' battle which left such a rankling memory behind.

APPENDIX[1]

THE TWO AFFIDAVITS FILED IN SUPPORT OF PLAINTIFF'S APPLICATION FOR INTERIM INJUNCTION IN "DICKENS v. LEE."

In Chancery

Between CHARLES DICKENS, *Plaintiff*

and

RICHARD EGAN LEE and JOHN HADDOCK, *Defendants*

CHARLES DICKENS of Number 1 Devonshire Terrace York Gate Regents Park in the parish of Saint Marylebone in the county of Middlesex maketh oath and saith That he this deponent is the author of several books which have been printed and published and very extensively sold and whereby this deponent has derived great pecuniary profits And that before the month of December One thousand eight hundred and forty three this deponent invented composed and wrote an original tale or book entitled "A Christmas Carol in Prose being a Ghost Story of Christmas" and that the same is a work of invention and fancy And that the subject and incidents thereof and the characters and personages therein introduced and described are of this deponent's sole invention And this deponent was and is the author and sole proprietor of the said book And that the whole property of and in and the sole right of printing and publishing the same was and has at all times been and still is vested in this deponent And this deponent further saith that he this deponent has duly caused the said book and this deponents proprietorship therein to be registered in the Book of Registry of the Stationers Company kept at the Hall of the said Company by the Officer appointed by the said Company in pursuance of and according to the directions in that behalf contained in the Act of Parliament of the fifth and sixth years of the reign of her present Majesty entitled "An Act to amend the law of Copyright" And that this Deponent caused his said Book to be printed And that

[1] Certain small clerical errors appearing in the affidavits are not repeated in this Appendix.

on the nineteenth day of December One thousand eight hundred and forty three the same was published by Messieurs Chapman and Hall of the Strand in the County of Middlesex as the agents and publishers of this deponent and on this deponent's behalf And this deponent further saith that the Book produced to this deponent at the time of making this affidavit and marked with the letter "A" is a copy of the book or work so as aforesaid written and composed by this deponent, and published as aforesaid And this deponent further saith that the said Book immediately upon its publication became extremely popular and that many copies thereof have been sold And that the same is still in course of publication and sale And this deponent further saith he has already made and received large profits thereby And that the same is of great value to this deponent as such sole owner and proprietor of the said book as aforesaid And that Richard Egan Lee and John Haddock who are the defendants in this suit have lately and without the permission or authority of this deponent made or procured to be made a colourable imitation of this deponent's said book and they have printed and published a part of such imitation and they threaten and intend to continue to print and publish the same and hereafter to print and publish a continuation thereof until they shall have completed their imitation of this deponent's said book And that such part of the said defendants' said publication as has been already published has been entitled by the said defendants "A Christmas Ghost Story re-originated from the original by Charles Dickens Esquire, and analytically condensed expressly for this work" and purports to form the 16th number of a work called "Parley's Illuminated Library" which is published weekly And that such last mentioned number was first printed and published by the said defendants on the sixth day of January last And that upon the wrapper of the same number is a note or advertisement in the terms following that is to say "This week is commenced and will be continued until complete, "A Christmas Ghost Story Re-originated from the original by Charles Dickens Esquire and analytically condensed expressly for this work" And this Deponent further saith that the book or work now produced and shewn to this deponent marked with the letter "B" is to the best of this deponent's belief a copy of such book or work so published by the said defendants And this deponent further saith that the said number which has been so already printed and published as aforesaid contains a colorable imitation of abcut one half of this deponent's said book And that the said publication of the said defendants is a mere piracy of this deponent's said book and that the subject characters personages and incidents of the defendants' said publication are taken from and are the same as those contained in this deponent's said work except that the name of one of the personages in this deponent's said book called "Fezziwig" is in the said defendants' publication called "Fuzziwig" And that in many instances the language of the said defendants' said publication is the same with that of this deponent's said work And that although in many other instances the language of the defendants' said work has been altered yet that such alteration has been only colorable and has been used for the purpose of endeavouring to conceal the fact that the defendants' said work has been copied or imitated from this deponent's said book And this deponent further saith that he first became acquainted with the fact of the said defendants having so as aforesaid published and printed a portion of his said work on Saturday the sixth day of January instant about the hour of three of the clock in the afternoon of that day when one of the printed copies of the defendants' said publication was sent to this deponent by Messieurs Bradbury and Evans the printers of this deponent and his attention was thereby called to the defendants' said publication That this deponent thereupon carefully looked into the copy of the work so as aforesaid published by the said defendants and contrasted same with a copy of his this deponent's own production and on doing so found the defendants' said publication to contain in many parts thereof a colorable imitation of one half of this deponent's said book That thereupon this deponent on Monday the eighth day of January instant gave instructions to his solicitor Mr. Thomas Mitton of Southampton Buildings Chancery Lane to take the necessary steps on his this deponent's behalf for obtaining an injunction to restrain the defendants from continuing to print publish and sell any portion of this deponent's said work And this deponent further saith he firmly believes and is fully persuaded that it is the intention of the said defendants to print publish and sell the residue of this deponent's said work unless restrained by the Order and Injunction of this Honorable Court

Sworn at the Public Office Southampton Buildings Chancery Lane this 9th day of January 1844 before me } CHARLES DICKENS.

S. DUCKWORTH.

[*Filed 9th January* 1844.]

In Chancery

Between Charles Dickens, *Plaintiff*

and

Richard Egan Lee and John Haddock, *Defendants*

Robert Bach Clerk to Thomas Mitton of 23 Southampton Buildings in the county of Middlesex solicitor for the above named plaintiff maketh oath and saith that the above named defendants carry on the business of printers at Craven Yard Drury Lane and that he this deponent did on the eighth day of January instant purchase of a clerk or shopman at the shop or warehouse of the above named defendants situate and being in Craven Yard Drury Lane in the county of Middlesex the book or work now produced and shewn to this deponent and marked with the letter B and called or known by the name of "Parley's Illuminated Library" No. 16 And this deponent further saith that he this deponent hath carefully examined and compared the said book or work marked B with a certain other book or work now produced and shewn to this deponent marked with the letter A and being a copy of a certain book written and published by the above named plaintiff and called "A Christmas Carol in prose being a Ghost Story of Christmas" And this deponent further saith that the said book marked B is a colourable imitation of about one half of the said plaintiff's book marked A and that the said publication of the said defendants marked B is as this deponent verily believes a mere piracy of the said plaintiff's said book marked A and that the subject characters personages and incidents of the defendants' said book marked B are taken from and are the same as those contained in the plaintiff's said book save that the name of one of the personages in the plaintiff's said book called Fezziwig is in the said defendant's said book called Fuzziwig and that in many instances the language of the said defendants' said book or publication is the same with that of the said plaintiff's said work And this deponent further saith that although in many other instances the language of the said defendants' said work has been altered yet that such alteration has been only colourable and has as this deponent verily believes been used for the purpose of endeavouring to conceal the fact that the said defendants' said work has been copied or imitated from the book of the said plaintiff And this deponent further saith that he this deponent hath underscored and marked in the margin of the said book marked B several of the passages thereof wherein the said defendants have followed the language of the above named plaintiff in his said book marked A and that in all other parts of the said book so published by the defendants the incidents and characters are the same and follow in the same order and detail as in the said book marked A.

ROBT. BACH. { Sworn at the Public Office Southampton Buildings in the County of Middlesex this ninth day of January 1844. Before me S. DUCKWORTH.

[*Filed 9th January* 1844.]

ORDER FOR INTERIM INJUNCTION IN "DICKENS *v.* LEE."

Vice-Chancellor KNIGHT BRUCE

Wednesday the 10*th day of January* 1844

Between CHARLES DICKENS, *Plaintiff*

and

RICHARD EGAN LEE and JOHN HADDOCK, *Defendants*

Upon opening the matter this present day unto this court by Mr. Bacon of counsel for the plaintiff it was alleged that it appears by the affidavit of the plaintiff Charles Dickens . . . that it appears by the affidavit of Robert Bach . . . to be relieved wherein and for an injunction the plaintiff hath exhibited his bill in this court against the said defendants as by the certificate of the Clerk of Records and Writs in whose division the cause appears And therefore it was prayed that the said defendants might be restrained by the order and injunction of this court from printing publishing selling or otherwise disposing of the publication in the plaintiffs bill named which had been commenced by them under the title of a "Christmas Ghost Story" as in the said bill mentioned or any continuation or other part thereof and from copying or imitating in the whole or in part the plaintiff's book entitled "A Christmas Carol in Prose" being a Ghost Story of Christmas in the plaintiff's bill also mentioned WHEREUPON and upon hearing the said affidavits and the Clerk of Records and Writs' certificate read THIS COURT DOTH ORDER that an injunction be awarded against the defendants

Richard Egan Lee and John Haddock to restrain them their servants workmen or agents from printing publishing selling or otherwise disposing of the publication in the plaintiff's bill mentioned which has been commenced by them under the title of "A Christmas Ghost Story" as in the said bill mentioned or any continuation or other part thereof and from copying or imitating[1] in the whole or in part the plaintiff's book entitled "A Christmas Carol in Prose being a Ghost Story of Christmas" in the plaintiff's bill also mentioned until the defendants shall fully answer the plaintiff's bill or this court make other order to the contrary. H. H.

REPORT OF HEARING OF MOTIONS FOR INTERIM INJUNCTION IN "DICKENS *v.* BERGER" AND THREE OTHER SUITS.

From "The Times" of Friday, the 12th of January 1844.

VICE-CHANCELLOR'S COURTS, THURSDAY, JANUARY 11.

(Before Sir J. K. BRUCE.)

Dickens v. *Berger—Same* v. *Clark—Same* v. *Strange—Same* v. *Cleave.*

Mr. Serjeant Talfourd moved for a special injunction, in each of the foregoing cases, on behalf of Mr. Charles Dickens, to restrain the several defendants from continuing an alleged piracy of the "Christmas Carol in Prose" by that author. The learned counsel said his Honour had granted a similar injunction yesterday against the printer for the same alleged piracy of the same work, and Mr. Dickens felt that he could not have adequate protection for his reputation or his property without seeking the aid of the Court to restrain the publication of the work now complained of by the defendants in each case. The case in which he should first move would be that of "Dickens *v.* Berger," and the subject-matter of the alleged piracy was the work by that gentleman he had already alluded to. The object of Mr. Dickens in that book was to seize upon the associations belonging to Christmas, and to embody them in a more permanent form, and to bring to bear the fund of informa-

[1] It appears by the *Jurist* report that on the 25th of January 1844 the vice-chancellor varied the terms of the injunction by striking out the words, "or imitating."

tion he possessed upon the genial influences which that season of the year was calculated to bring forth. The book was published at 5*s.*, was illustrated with plates, and very quickly, as might have been anticipated, proved eminently successful. The main scope of the work was as follows: An aged man, not disfigured by any absolute or glaring vices, had grown old in the habit of money-getting, and who was not open to the genial influences of the Christmas season, the author caused to be visited by the spirit of Christmas past, Christmas present, and Christmas to come; the effect produced by which visit was, that he became, not a sadder, but a wiser man. This outline of his work the author filled up by placing the old man again among the scenes of his youth; showing him his schoolboy days, his boyish apprentice hours, his early love—a love only blighted by his own worship of mammon; and then, by contrast, disclosing the various scenes of happiness passing around him; taking him to see his nephew whom he had cast off, to show how happy even he could be under all the ills of adverse fortune, and then taking him to the residence of his old clerk, to behold how well he and his family could enjoy the happiness of Christmas even under the circumstances of poverty. This idea had been adopted in a work called "Parley's Illuminated Library," being a series of essays published either weekly or monthly, and Mr. Dickens had to complain that it was so printed as to render it doubtful whether or not that gentleman was engaged in conducting it. The announcement was thus: "This work is commenced, and will be continued till complete"—a thing very likely to happen, for already two-thirds of the alleged piracy had appeared. It was called, "A Ghost Story, reiterated and reconstructed from a Christmas Carol in Prose, by Charles Dickens, Esquire, and analytically condensed expressly for this work." The object evidently was to induce the purchasers at 2*d.* to believe that they had for that sum what they could not regularly obtain for less than 5*s.* The learned Serjeant, in reply to an observation of his Honour, said that that would be having the work of Mr. Dickens cheaper than in a review. The plate in the piracy was not taken from Mr. Dickens's publication, but it was ingeniously made to relate to something to occur in the following number. The piracy stopped at the Christmas dinner of the poor clerk, at that particular point where the goose having been introduced, expectation was alive and at the utmost stretch for the appearance of the pudding. The last words of the number were: "All was eager expectation." The goose was on table, but the pudding had not arrived, and in order to give zest to the anticipation, the plate represented its introduction blazing in brandy, received with acclamation and in the triumph of successful cookery. The learned counsel had attentively read the alleged piracy, the original he had already had the pleasure of perusing; and the effect produced on his mind was that the only difference between the two works was, that the language of the piracy was in some places condensed, and in others amplified in a manner which must be anything but flattering or satisfactory to Mr. Dickens. The scenes were the same, the incidents alike, and with one trifling variation of spelling, the names of the characters identical. With the single exception that the alleged piracy was altered so as to be upon a level with the capacity of its presumed readers, he could see no dissimilarity between the two works. The learned counsel then pointed out to the Court various passages in the two books, showing immaterial alterations, immaterial at least excepting as to their inferiority in the alleged pirated work. The scheme of the fable was exactly the same, the names the same, with the solitary exception of the introduction of one additional letter into one of them. One of the mottoes attached to the alleged piracy was suggested to have been taken from Sheridan; it ran, "Illustrated, embellished, enlarged, and elaborately ornamented." He thought he could furnish the publisher with a more appropriate quotation from the witty author, where he says in the "School for Scandal," "You use my ideas as Gipsies do stolen children; they steal children, disfigure them, and then make them pass for their own."

His Honour inquired whether the defendant was identified with the Berger whose name appeared on the cover of the book?

Mr. Bacon said he was amply so in the affidavits filed in support of the motion. There was no regular publisher of the work, but there were several names on the wrapper, of whom it was announced the same could be purchased. The copy in each case was purchased from each of the defendants.

His Honour.—I think there is sufficient for the present purpose. You may take the injunction.

THE FIVE AFFIDAVITS FILED ON BEHALF OF DEFENDANTS IN "DICKENS *v.* LEE."

In Chancery

Between Charles Dickens, *Plaintiff*

and

Richard Egan Lee and John Haddock, *Defendants*

Richard Egan Lee of Craven Yard Drury Lane in the parish of Saint Clement Danes in the county of Middlesex printer and publisher one of the above named Defendants maketh oath and saith that he this deponent is the managing partner of the firm of Lee and Haddock printers and publishers the Defendants hereto That this deponent has for many years been engaged in the editing of his own and other newspapers and literary periodicals That in the year one thousand eight hundred and forty one this deponent commenced a certain work entitled "Parley's Library or Treasury of Knowledge Entertainment and Delight" and did then and thereafter in conjunction with his coadjutor Mr. Henry Hewitt a gentleman of considerable experience and talent write arrange complete and publish nine volumes of the said work That in the first volume of the said work which was published before Christmas in the said year one thousand eight hundred and forty one a copy of which said volume is produced and shewn to this Deponent at the time of swearing this his affidavit and marked C this Deponent's said coadjutor Henry Hewitt did analyse abridge reoriginate and publish two of the plaintiff's well known and then recently published works entitled respectively "The Old Curiosity Shop" and "Barnaby Rudge" That at page 278 of the said volume of "Parley's Library" marked C there is a commentary upon the plaintiff's merits as an author also written by the said Henry Hewitt That to the said volume in which the said analyses abridgments and reoriginations of said plaintiff's said works were published this Deponent wrote a dedication of the said volume to the said plaintiff which said dedication was and is printed at the back of the title page of every copy of the said volume That a great number to the extent of seventy thousand at the least of some parts of the said volume were printed and published by this Deponent and that in addition to such extensive circulation and public notoriety of the said work this Deponent did moreover before Christmas one thousand eight hundred and forty one write an autograph inscription of his this

Deponent's respectful compliments to the plaintiff upon a blank leaf in a copy of the said volume and marked C and did transmit such copy to the plaintiff who as this Deponent verily believes received the said copy and was thereby made perfectly cognizant and aware of the analysation abridgment and reorigination in this Deponent's said work of his the plaintiff's said works respectively entitled "The Old Curiosity Shop" and "Barnaby Rudge" That the plaintiff never in any way interfered to prevent the publication or circulation of this Deponent's said volume nor ever as this Deponent verily believes expressed disapprobation of the said analyses That the express purpose of this Deponent's said work was and is avowed to be to impart in a familiar style synoptical sketches of all works of value in ancient or modern literature That in pursuance of such avowed purpose certain other of the plaintiff's works or productions have been from time to time analysed and reproduced in this Deponent's said work entitled "Parley's Library" while some other of the plaintiff's productions have not been noticed at all in the said work such others so unnoticed being deemed by this Deponent and his coadjutor to be of unequal or inferior merit and pretensions That besides such works of the plaintiff as are hereinbefore mentioned the books or works of other eminent authors including Joanna Baillie Mrs. Gore Captain Marryat Sir Edward Lytton Bulwer Lord Byron Messieurs Moore Lockhart Campbell Cooper James Warren and very many other distinguished writers have been in like manner systematically and as this Deponent verily believes honestly and fairly reoriginated by close analysis and condensation of plot and incident in this Deponent's said work entitled "Parley's Library" And this Deponent verily believes that no complaint has at any time been made by any of the said authors of this Deponent's treatment of their works That soon after the publication of the plaintiff's book entitled "A Christmas Carol in prose being a ghost story of Christmas" this deponent in the exercise of his usual avocations and in accordance with the general custom of editors did critically examine the plaintiff's last mentioned work That the opinion and notes of this Deponent resulting from such examination of the plaintiff's said work were communicated by this Deponent to his said coadjutor Henry Hewitt who proceeded to abridge and analytically condense the said "Christmas Carol in Prose" That the said Henry Hewitt did by the exercise of much skill talent and invention reoriginate in brief the plaintiff's last mentioned work That this Deponent received the entire manuscript of the abridgment or reproduction thereof from the said Henry Hewitt before the first day of this present month of January That this Deponent thereupon proceeded at the said Henry Hewitt's earnest request to compare and examine the plaintiff's said work and the said manuscript abridgment thereof that this Deponent was completely satisfied and convinced that the said Henry Hewitt had skilfully and fairly exercised his own mental powers in such abridgment and this Deponent thereupon gave orders for the immediate illustration and publication of the said manuscript by the same work as is complained of by the plaintiff's Bill in this cause That one George Stiff an artist of great reputation and distinguished talent invented and designed three engravings from the said Henry Hewitt's manuscript for the said abridgment or condensed reproduction entitled " A Christmas Ghost Story reoriginated from the original by Charles Dickens Esquire and analytically condensed expressly for this work " That the said title was penned by this Deponent and intended to express what this Deponent verily believes to be the fact that very considerable improvements and in some instances large original additions as well as condensation had been effected by the said Henry Hewitt in the machinery of the said tale as for example in plaintiff's said work one of the personages called Tiny Tim is merely described as having sung a song about a child being lost in the snow whereas in the said Henry Hewitt's said manuscript an original carol or song of sixty lines was written by the said Henry Hewitt for the said personage called Tiny Tim a copy of which said song is given in the paper marked B and is in this Deponent's opinion admirably adapted to the occasion and replete with pathos and poetry That many other instances might be cited wherein the said Henry Hewitt in his said manuscript abridgment or reproduction of the plaintiff's said work made wise and judicious alterations of and departures from the incidents style and plot of the plaintiff's work That so far from the said Defendants' said publication being (as charged in the plaintiff's bill) a colorable imitation of the plaintiff's said work or any part thereof this Deponent verily believes that numerous incongruities in the plaintiff's work involving the unhinging of the whole story or plot and some of which incongruities this Deponent had noted to the said Henry Hewitt on commencing his the said Henry Hewitt's said work have been tastefully remedied therein by the extended critical experience of dramatic effect and the ready perception of harmonies possessed by the said Henry Hewitt That Henry Hewitt is not only an author and writer of great ability but a man of undoubted probity and integrity That this Deponent has had the highest testimonials to the general character of said Henry Hewitt which were signed by men of the highest standing in the literary world as well as by many distinguished clergymen magistrates merchants bankers and members of both Houses of Parliament That from this Deponent's knowledge of the said Henry Hewitt's writings he this Deponent is of opinion that the plaintiff is indebted for the germs of many of his the said plaintiff's works to the hints of the said Henry Hewitt and particularly in reference to the plaintiff's said work entitled "A Christmas Carol in Prose being a Ghost Story of Christmas" this Deponent verily believes that the plaintiff first derived the original suggestion for that work from certain criticisms written by the said Henry Hewitt and inserted in this Deponent's said work entitled "Parley's Library" in one of which said criticisms upon a paper by the plaintiff entitled "The Last of the Lamplighters" allusion is particularly made to the plaintiff's happy peculiarity of expressing dreamy and shadowy indistinctness That a considerable outlay of money was required to produce the said Defendants' said publication entitled "A Christmas Ghost Story" That Defendants might by adopting the system of copious extracts which is permitted to many periodical works of far higher price and pretensions than the said Defendants' publication have got up at a very trifling expense a mere mechanical abridgment of the plaintiff's said work That No. 17 of "Parleys Illuminated Library" also produced and shewn and marked B ought to and of right should and would have been published on the thirteenth of this present month of January if the injunction had not been granted by this Honorable Court That the actual loss and damage sustained by this Deponent and his said co-partner from the restraint of such publication by the injunction granted by this Honorable Court amounts to a serious and considerable sum and Deponent solemnly avers that unless this injunction be forthwith dissolved the pecuniary loss to this Deponent and his said co-partner from the continued restraint of the said publication No. 17 will be ruinous and wholly irreparable.

RICHARD EGAN LEE.	Sworn at the Chancery Affidavit Office Symonds Inn in the County of Middlesex this sixteenth day of January 1844 Before me

S. ANDERDON.

[*Filed* 16*th January* 1844]

In Chancery

Between Charles Dickens, *Plaintiff*
and
Richard Egan Lee and John Haddock, *Defendants*

Henry Hewitt of Number 101 White Lion Street Islington in the County of Middlesex author and editor maketh oath and saith that he this deponent has been for thirty five years engaged in Literary pursuits and that he can produce numerous testimonials from persons of high station in Literature and Society having reference to his ability as a writer and the general integrity of his character That this deponent would hold in utter disdain the meanness of copying and employing as his own the ideas and modes of expression of any author living or dead That this deponent is a writer employed by the above named defendants and receiving for his services a considerable salary That he is the writer of a certain paper or tale entitled " A Christmas Ghost Story reoriginated from the original by Charles Dickens Esquire " being the publication and intended publication of the defendants hereto produced and shewn to this deponent at the time of swearing this affidavit and marked A and B charged by the Plaintiff as being a colorable imitation of his the said plaintiff's work entitled " A Christmas Carol in Prose being a Ghost Story of Christmas " That this deponent in his capacity of Joint Editor of " Parley's Illuminated Library " received from Richard Egan Lee before the twenty fifth day of December last a copy of the plaintiff's said work together with sundry notes and memoranda pointing out certain beauties and many defects and inconsistencies in the Plaintiff's said work That this deponent then in accordance with his custom for many years past proceeded to analyse the plaintiff's said work for the purpose of reoriginating the tale or plot thereof in an abridged and a synoptical form That besides the defects or wants of harmony pointed out by the said Richard Egan Lee this deponent detected so many others as to induce him in numerous instances to abandon the plot of the plaintiff's said tale and to substitute what this deponent verily believes to be a more artistical style of expression and of incident That this deponent could had he been so disposed have cut the plaintiff's said work into fragments and then effected a flimsy reunion by tacking together such fragments with a few thread-like sentences as the custom is in many periodical works of far higher price and pretensions than the said publication of the defendants but that such a mode would as deponent verily believes be rather mutilation than abridgment or reorigination That this deponent has at times analytically reoriginated several works of the plaintiff and among others two entitled "The Old Curiosity Shop" and "Barnaby Rudge" That a copy of the volume containing such analytical re-originations and condensations of the incidents of the plaintiff's said two works is produced to this deponent at the time of his swearing this affidavit and marked C That this deponent saw a manuscript inscription to the plaintiff written by the said Defendant Richard Egan Lee previously to Christmas one thousand eight hundred and forty one upon a blank or fly leaf of a copy of the said volume marked C produced and shewn to the deponent at the time of swearing this affidavit That this deponent's son William Hewitt took the said volume to the residence of the said plaintiff That the said William Hewitt is not at present in London but that deponent entertains no doubt whatever that the Plaintiff received the said copy of that volume That the Plaintiff never in any way interfered to suppress the publication of the said analytical reproductions of his said works That deponent verily believes that such abridgments materially augmented the sale of the original works That this deponent on divers and numerous occasions expressed his honest opinion of the plaintiff's merits as an Author and a writer of fiction That this deponent verily believes the plaintiff has however unconsciously been indebted to the critical remarks made from time to time by this deponent in said "Parley's Library" for the germ of more than one of his productions And this deponent also verily believes the plaintiff to be far more indebted to the works of an author named Washington Irving for the material of his "Christmas Carol" than this deponent is indebted to the plaintiff in his the deponent's said Abridgment That this deponent's avowed purpose in his analytical abridgments of the works of popular writers is exemplified in an extract from this deponent's address on the commencement of the said work entitled "Parley's Library" that is to say "The rich and costly stores of the illustrious never-dying few of whose works vast numbers of the youth of both sexes never heard will be popularly presented by an occasional analysis of some celebrated author thus affording we trust such an introduction as will engender fierce and irrepressible desire to become more intimately acquainted with the productions of these master-spirits affording healthy incitement to steady application at the sources whence our own materials are derived and alluring youth to exercise their own powers in producing an analysis of every book worthy of recollection a process which while furnishing a subject will throw them upon their individual resources for language That this deponent verily believes that the humbler classes of this Kingdom have neither time nor money to expend upon large and high priced works That the conveyance of faithful pictures in miniature of expensive works is and for many years has been this deponent's study and practice That this deponent in dealing with the plaintiff's tale or any other author's works has always candidly laid bare its quality and that on the present occasion this deponent has in the honest exercise of his judgment in numerous particulars wholly abandoned the plot of the plaintiff's said work in order to improve the tale and render the same the more consistent and to give greater effect to the leading incidents therein That this deponent gave his said manuscript to one George Stiff an artist of repute for the purpose of illustration That three illustrations were furnished by the said George Stiff of which together with the concluding printed copy of it this deponent's said manuscript a copy of which was produced and shewn to this deponent at the time of swearing this affidavit and marked B That this deponent verily believes for the reasons hereinbefore adduced and many other reasons which he is ready to substantiate that the plaintiff's said work is not only not colorably imitated by this deponent in the publication by the defendants but that there has been an entire abandonment of the plaintiff's work in all that can be deemed its essentials.

HENRY HEWITT.	Sworn at the Chancery Affidavit Office Symonds Inn in the County of Middlesex this sixteenth day of January 1844 Before me S. ANDERDON.

[*Filed* 16*th January* 1844]

In Chancery

Between CHARLES DICKENS, *Plaintiff*

and

RICHARD EGAN LEE and JOHN HADDOCK, *Defendants*

GEORGE STIFF of No. 16 Gloucester Place Camden Town in the county of Middlesex maketh oath and saith that he is and for many years has been an artist draughtsman and engraver That before the first day of the present month of January he designed invented and engraved three several illustrations for a certain publication or work intended to be published by the said defendants entitled "A Christmas Ghost Story" That the impressions or proofs of those three engravings or illustrations so solely designed invented and engraved by this deponent are identical with and the same as the illustrations or engravings in the numbers of the defendants' said intended publication and respectively marked A and B and produced and shewn to deponent at the time of swearing this affidavit That this deponent has never read the plaintiff's work entitled "A Christmas Carol in prose being a Ghost Story of Christmas" nor did he this deponent ever in any way or manner examine the plates or illustrations of the plaintiffs said work but that he received the manuscripts of the defendants' said intended publication which was required to be illustrated from Mr. Henry Hewitt whom this deponent verily believes to be the writer thereof as in times past and on divers and numerous occasions this deponent has been in the habit of receiving other manuscripts from the said Henry Hewitt for the purpose of illustrating such manuscripts by original designs and engravings That this deponent has since the granting of the present injunction against the defendants carefully compared the illustrations in the plaintiff's said work with his this deponent's own engravings in the publication of the defendants and verily believes that there is no figure character scene or personage in the plaintiff's said work at all resembling any figure character scene or personage in this deponent's said engravings so invented and designed by this deponent from the said manuscripts of the said Henry Hewitt That he this deponent received from the present defendants a considerable sum of money for such three inventions designs and engravings and that this deponent verily believes the defendants to be wholly incapable of knowingly infringing on the copyright or property of any author whatever inasmuch as this deponent has frequently heard the said defendants express their decided disapprobation of the practice or system of wholesale verbatim extract with short connecting paragraphs which this deponent alleges and verily believes to prevail in many Literary Journals Reviews and other works of considerably higher price and pretentions than those of the said defendants' work entitled Parleys Illuminated Library That this deponent verily believes from his experience that the tendency of such rewritten abridgments and productions of popular works as the defendants have published or intended to publish are not only beneficial to the public but by enhancing the popularity of the original author contribute in many ways to such author's pecuniary benefit as this deponent verily believes was the case with a certain work entitled "Masterman Ready or the Wreck of the Pacific" written by Captain Marryat and analysed and reproduced in the same way as the present intended publication by the defendants and also a certain other work entitled "The Last of the Barons" by Sir Edward Lytton Bulwer and in numerous other instances which this deponent can adduce And this deponent further believes that by the abridged reproduction of the plaintiff's said work in the candid manner set forth in the title of the defendants' tale a positive benefit instead of injury as charged would be conferred on the said plaintiff's copyright and reputation.

GEO^E. STIFF.	Sworn at the Chancery Affidavit Office Symonds Inn in the County of Middlesex this sixteenth day of January 1844.

[*Filed* 16*th January* 1844]

In Chancery

Between CHARLES DICKENS, *Plaintiff*

and

RICHARD EGAN LEE and JOHN HADDOCK, *Defendants*

GEORGE MUDIE of No. — Stanhope Street Strand in the county of Middlesex Gentleman maketh oath and saith that he has carefully perused the Work published by the above named defendants under the title of "A Christmas Ghost Story reoriginated from the original by Charles Dickens Esquire and analytically condensed expressly for this work" now produced and shewn to this Deponent at the time of swearing this affidavit marked A and against the publication of which an Injunction has been obtained by the plaintiff That this Deponent was for many years Chief Editor of the Sun daily newspaper and has devoted more than thirty years to Literary pursuits and has obtained considerable reputation as an Author of numerous works in Philology and Political Economy and as a writer of works of poetry and fiction which have been very extensively circulated That the Deponent's practice and study for so many years have enabled him to form a judgment upon the matters in question in this cause That he has compared the work published by the defendants with the work written by the said Charles Dickens entitled "A Christmas Carol in prose being a Ghost Story of Christmas" and is of opinion that there is not the slightest ground for denominating the said work so published by the said defendants a colourable imitation of piracy of the plaintiff's said work inasmuch as although the characters and some of the incidents contained in the said book so published by the said defendants are avowedly derived from the original of the said Charles Dickens as appears on the title in the number of the said work produced and shewn to deponent and marked A yet the difference of thought style matter and quantity of the two works many of the best parts of each not being in the other and the extreme disparity of price between the publication by the defendants and the work written by the plaintiff could not by any possibility allow of the abridgment being taken or sold for the original but as this deponent verily believes so far from the defendants' said publication injuring or being calculated to injure the sale of the plaintiff's said work he this deponent has invariably found that the treating of works of this deponent and of others in like manner as the said defendants have treated the plaintiff's book has not been injurious to the said works so treated but on the contrary this deponent is well convinced that the popularity created by the abridgments reviews or analyses have in all such cases added to the sale of the originals And this deponent not only verily believes and declares from his own knowledge that the condensation or abridgment by the defendants of a former work by the plaintiff entitled "The Old Curiosity Shop" of which said condensation or abridgment this deponent has been informed by the publisher thereof and verily believes that more than fifty thousand copies were circulated did most materially contribute to the popularity and consequent pecuniary benefit of the plaintiff by enhancing the demand for his the plaintiffs original work entitled "Master Humphrey's Clock" That the many years which this deponent has spent in literary engagements have given him certain knowledge of the nature of Public Opinion and from which this deponent is well assured that the readers of the publication by the defendants which is sold at the price of one penny and those of the work written by the plaintiff which is sold at the price of five shillings belong to a totally different class And this deponent is also assured that the persons who have purchased the said work of the defendants would not have purchased the work published by the plaintiff That the publication by the defendants being intended for and in fact purchased by those whose circumstances prevent them not only from purchasing but for the most part from even hiring a work of higher price is calculated to add to the popularity of the plaintiff as well as to confer benefit upon Society.

GEORGE MUDIE.	Sworn at the Chancery Affidavit Office Symonds Inn in the County of Middlesex this sixteenth day of January 1844 Before me S. ANDERDON.

[*Filed* 16*th January* 1844]

In Chancery

Between CHARLES DICKENS, *Plaintiff*

and

RICHARD EGAN LEE and JOHN HADDOCK, *Defendants*

EDWARD LEMAN BLANCHARD of No. 7 Clements Inn Strand in the County of Middlesex Gentleman maketh Oath and Saith that he has devoted many years to literary pursuits and has attained considerable success and profit as a dramatic author and a writer of works of romance and fiction That he has carefully perused the work published by the above named Defendants produced and shewn to this Deponent at the time of swearing this affidavit and marked A under the title of " A Christmas Ghost Story reoriginated from the original by Charles Dickens Esquire and analytically condensed expressly for this work " and against the publication of which an injunction has been obtained by the Plaintiff That this Deponent's practice and study for so many years have enabled him to form a judgment upon the matters in question in this Cause That he has compared the work published by the Defendants with the work written by the Plaintiff and is of opinion that there is not the slightest ground for denominating the said work so published by the Defendants a colorable imitation or piracy of the said work by the Plaintiff inasmuch as although the characters and some of the incidents contained in the said book so published by the Defendants are avowedly derived from the Original of the Plaintiff as appears on the title in the number of the said Work marked A yet the difference of style matter and quantity of the two works many of the best part of each not being in the other and the extreme disparity of price between the publication of the Defendants and the work written by the Plaintiff would effectually prevent the said abridgment from being taken or sold for the original but as this Deponent verily believes the Defendants' said Publication will materially contribute to the popularity of and consequent demand for the Plaintiff's work entitled "A Christmas Carol in prose being a Ghost Story of Christmas" which said Work as well as others of the said Plaintiff's publications are very similar in many parts and passages to Washington Irving's Works That the many years which this Deponent has spent in literary engagements have given him certain knowledge of the nature of public opinion and from which this Deponent is well assured that the readers of the publication of the said Defendants which is sold at the price of one penny and that those of the work written by the Plaintiff which is sold at the price of five shillings belong to a totally different class of Society and this Deponent is also assured that the persons who have purchased the said Work of the Defendants would not have purchased the work published by the Plaintiff That the Publication by the Defendants being intended for and in fact purchased by those whose circumstances prevent them not only from purchasing but for the most part from even hiring a book of higher price is calculated in this Deponent's opinion to add to the popularity of the Plaintiff as well as to confer benefit upon society.

EDWARD LEMAN BLANCHARD. { Sworn at the Chancery Affidavit Office Symonds Inn in the County of Middlesex this seventeenth day of January 1844 Before me

S. ANDERDON.

[*Filed 17th January* 1844]

AFFIDAVIT OF DICKENS FILED IN REPLY IN "DICKENS *v.* LEE"

In Chancery

Between CHARLES DICKENS, *Plaintiff*

and

RICHARD EGAN LEE and JOHN HADDOCK, *Defendants*

CHARLES DICKENS of No. 1 Devonshire Terrace York Gate, Regents Park in the County of Middlesex Esquire maketh oath and saith that he has perused an affidavit of Richard Egan Lee made in this cause and sworn the sixteenth day of January one thousand eight hundred and forty four and also an affidavit of Henry Hewitt also made in this cause and sworn on the said sixteenth day of January one thousand eight hundred and forty four And this Deponent says that on the fourth of January one thousand eight hundred and forty two this Deponent quitted England for the United States of America and remained absent from England from the time last mentioned until the month of June one thousand eight hundred and forty two And this Deponent denies that before Christmas one thousand eight hundred and forty one or at any other time this Deponent did receive any copy of the volume in the said Affidavits respectively mentioned and therein mentioned to be marked C to the best of this deponent's knowledge remembrance or belief And this Deponent positively saith that if he this Deponent did receive any such book from the said Defendant Richard Egan Lee that he this deponent never read the same or that this Deponent was thereby made perfectly or in any way cognisant or aware of the alleged analysation abridgment or reorigination in the said Affidavits respectively mentioned of this Deponent's works respectively entitled "The Old Curiosity Shop" and "Barnaby Rudge" in the same affidavits mentioned or of either of them And this Deponent says that in the month of February one thousand eight hundred and forty two this Deponent being then at a Public Entertainment in the City of Boston in America a printed copy of a printed copy of an unauthorised version of this Deponent's said work called "The Old Curiosity Shop" and which printed copy purported to have been published in England was shewn to this Deponent by Doctor Palfrey of Boston aforesaid but this deponent says that he looked but cursorily at the said printed copy which was shewn to him as aforesaid and that he did not at the time last mentioned or at any other time read the last mentioned printed copy nor had he any notice or knowledge of the nature or contents thereof save from the same having been shewn to him by the said Doctor Palfrey as aforesaid and from this Deponent having so cursorily looked at the same as aforesaid And this Deponent does not know whether or not the said printed copy so shewn to him as last aforesaid was a copy of the said volume marked C in the said affidavits mentioned or any part thereof But save as aforesaid this Deponent according to the best of his recollection and belief denies that he has at any time seen or read any copy of the said volume marked C as aforesaid or any part thereof And this Deponent says that he has never at any time sanctioned or knowingly permitted the Defendants or any other person to copy or imitate either his work in the Bill filed in this cause mentioned or the works in the said affidavits mentioned or either of them but this Deponent says that as soon as he became acquainted with the fact that such infringement of this Deponent's property as in the said Bill is complained of came to this Deponent's knowledge he took such proceedings to prevent the same as in this Deponent's former Affidavit filed in this cause is mentioned.

CHARLES DICKENS. { Sworn at the Public Office Southampton Buildings in the County of Middlesex this 17th day of January 1844 Before me W. WINGFIELD.

[*Filed 17th January* 1844]

REPORT OF HEARING OF DEFENDANTS' MOTION TO DISSOLVE INJUNCTION IN "DICKENS *v.* LEE."

From "The Times" of Friday, the 19th of January 1844.

VICE-CHANCELLOR'S COURTS, THURSDAY, JAN. 18.

(Before Sir J. K. BRUCE.)

Dickens v. *Lee.*[1]

Mr. Anderdon moved to dissolve the injunction granted on the 11th (*sic*) inst. restraining the defendant from copying or imitating the whole or any part of the *Christmas Carols in Prose* of Mr. Dickens, in the work called *Parley's Illuminated Magazine.* He contended that the defendant had done no more than he had a right to do, for that great labour, pains, and expense had been gone to in rewriting the work in question. No colourable inversion of the order of incidents had been resorted to, no concealment that the tale was borrowed from Mr. Dickens had been attempted, nor had any act been done which could in any manner be considered as an injury to Mr. Dickens in his reputation or profit. So far from there being any attempt to make the public believe that for 1*d.* they were buying what this eminent author had written and published at 5*s.*, the defendant in his work had a dedication of his labours to

[1] Printed "Berger" in the Report.

Mr. Dickens himself. In that dedication he did ample justice to Mr. Dickens's merit, and stated that his object was to afford the humbler and the junior classes of readers the means of perusing the forcible incidents which he had depicted ; and it was impossible to suppose that any injury could accrue to him, since no one who would read *Parley's Magazine* could be expected to go to the expense of the elegant volume of Mr. Dickens. The defendant had for some time been in the habit of abridging, condensing, reconstructing, or re-originating, or by whatever name the process could be aptly designated, the works of Mr. Dickens, as they issued from the press, in the book now complained of ; and yet Mr. Dickens, who, either by himself or his publishers, must have been aware of such proceeding, never took any steps, either at law or in equity, to put a stop to the practice. It was rather hard now that he should all of a sudden endeavour to interpose the authority of the Court of Chancery, in the middle of a work, after he had so long acquiesced in what the defendant had so done. The learned counsel then proceeded to read affidavits in support of his motion. In part of them the practice of publishing cheap editions of valuable works was enlarged upon as one of great benefit to the public.

His Honour said he thought that the position of the utility and value of cheap editions of works containing interesting and good information among the less wealthy classes of the community was one universally admitted. He knew at least of two publications [1] in this country in which such small-priced issues of good works had taken place, and the practice had been followed in countries abroad where it would have least been expected, and printed in languages as unlikely to have been supposed, and with the most beneficial effect.

Mr. Anderdon.—The question for the Court to say was whether, looking fairly and dispassionately at the two works, the defendant had bestowed so much mental labour on his, that, although admitted to be borrowed in idea, incidents, and names, from that of the plaintiff, he was justified in the course he had adopted, and whether he was not entitled to have the injunction against him dissolved. In the case of "Dodsley *v.* Kinnersley," 1 Ambler, 423, the beautiful tale of *Rasselas* had been printed without the moral reflections, and the publication was protected, at least the injunction to stop it failed.

[1] His Honour was presumably referring to *Chambers's Journal*, and *Knight's Penny Magazine*.

His Honour.—The incidents in *Rasselas* might be compressed in half a page. Story, properly speaking, there is none. In days when I was a novel reader I have often been disappointed at reading an old novel in a new dress. Times, country, names altered, but the incidents the same. This is the first time that I have met with a case in which all these are taken, and the language only altered. Has any complaint ever come before the Court of the adaptation of plots from novels for the purposes of the stage?

Mr. Anderdon was not aware.

His Honour.—Sir Walter Scott's novels were brought out as plays.

Mr. Serjeant Talfourd.—Yes, and with his permission, and dramatised with his sanction by Mr. Chambers. There was the case of the *Iron Chest*, of which complaint was made, and that was performed during the existence of Mr. Godwin's copyright in *Caleb Williams.*

Mr. Anderdon.—On the two grounds that this was not a colourable imitation of the plaintiff's book, and that it was no piracy, but that it fell within the case of "Dodsley *v.* Kinnersley," namely, that a fair application of mind and talent had been made to the labours of another by a new author, so as to render the publication a new thing, the injunction ought to be dissolved. So far from there being any *animus furandi,* all had been fair and open.

His Honour.—A man is not the less robbed because you tell him you rob him.

Mr. Anderdon.—The defendant has neither taken his valuable property nor has he injured his reputation. On the contrary, the defendant has done all in his power to add to the already justly-acquired fame of Mr. Dickens, and that gentleman ought to be proud that his writings find their way among classes who would not be elevated by their moral, or entertained by their forcible, scenes, were the publication of his works confined to such a price as 5*s*.

His Honour.—There are many who only read to talk, and a man who could be enabled to talk for 1*d*. would hardly give 5*s*. for the same gratification.

Mr. Anderdon.—Mr. Dickens ought to be sent to his remedy at law. If a jury should decide that he had sustained any damage let them have the opportunity of saying so, and to what amount; but so expensive a proceeding as a Chancery suit for a matter so trivial ought not to be endured. If he is degraded in his reputation, and injured in his means, let a jury say to what extent. Seeing that Mr. Dickens had acquiesced in a similar treatment of his former works in the same publication, and by the same publisher, he (Mr. Anderdon) called upon the Court to dissolve the injunction.

His Honour.—Show me any incident in *Parley's Magazine* different from one in Mr. Dickens's book.

Mr. Anderdon referred to the scene relating to the goose being sent for from the baker's.

His Honour.—That is rather an extension of a dialogue for the purpose of threatening an incident than an actual incident.

Mr. Anderdon then made some observations as to the form of the injunction.

Mr. Shebbeare supported the motion. He contended that talent, labour, and expense had been bestowed on the work complained of. *Parley's Magazine* was partly an abridgment, and partly a new work. Mr. Dickens, not having complained of former " re-originations, condensations, and analysations " of his other books, was not now to be heard respecting this.

Mr. Serjeant Talfourd and Mr. Bacon, who appeared to show cause against the motion, were not called upon.

His Honour said—The plaintiff in this case is the author and owner of a work of fiction, the copyright of which it is not contended is not properly the subject of protection in this court. The defendant has printed and published a novel, of which the fable, the persons, the names of persons, the characters, the age and time, and scene and country, are wholly the same. The style of language in which the story is told is in some instances identical, and in all similar. The exceptions to the similarity are when an idea is altered either by way of extension, or contraction, or substitution. Whether these alterations have made the new work more or less valuable, I am not called on to give an opinion. It is said that this is the case of an abridgment, and to be protected. I am not at present aware that one man has a right to abridge the work of another, nor do I mean to say that there may not lawfully be an abridgment, or that an abridgment would not be protected. How this may be, it is not for me here and now to say; but I do say, that to assert that one man has a right to abridge the work of another is going beyond what I believe the law to be. Lord Eldon, in " Wilkins *v.* Aikin," 17 Vesey, 426, said—" The question upon the whole is, whether this is a legitimate use of the plaintiff's publication in the fair exercise of a mental operation, deserving the character of an original work." I am clearly disposed to think that the present is not a legitimate use of Mr. Dickens's publication, that it is not a fair exercise of a mental operation, nor does it deserve the character of an original work. In no point does the defendant's publication meet the exigency pointed out by the guarded language of Lord Eldon. On the contrary, it appears to me to be a mere borrowing, with alterations and adaptations merely, and plainly colourable. Then it is said that the difference of price renders the mischief, if any, merely nominal for all practical purposes. The man who sustains a loss is he who has the best right to say whether the loss is prejudicial or not to him. The plaintiff has a property, and he has a right to say whether it is to be protected from the invasion of another. Whatever the difference of price, many instances might be mentioned in which the most material damage might ensue as a subject of property, and that is the only way in which the case can be presented here. Lord Eldon, in the judgment I have quoted, goes on—" The effect, I have no doubt, is prejudicial: it does not follow that therefore there is a breach of the legal right; but where that is so, and there is a fair question, the injunction ought not to be dissolved; but, according to the usual course, maintaining an injunction, an action should be brought forthwith." The injunction must be continued, an action must be brought, and the plaintiff must undertake to abide by any order the Court may make in case the injunction should be ultimately dissolved.

Mr. Anderdon said, that within a week the defendant would let the plaintiff know whether he would acquiesce in the continuance of the injunction.

REPORT OF FURTHER HEARING OF MOTION TO DISSOLVE INJUNCTION.

From "The Times" of 26th January 1844.

VICE-CHANCELLOR'S COURTS, THURSDAY, JANUARY 15.

Dickens v. *Lee.*

The injunction in this case, which was issued on the 11th inst., and which was to restrain the defendants, their servants, workmen, and agents, from printing, publishing, selling, or otherwise disposing of the publication in the bill mentioned, which had been commenced by them under the title of *Christmas Ghost Story*, or any continuation or other part thereof, and from copying or imitating, in the whole or in part, the complainant's book, entitled *A Christmas Carol in prose*, being a Ghost Story of Christmas, was varied by the omission of the words "or imitate."

Mr. Serjeant Talfourd and Mr. Bacon said that the plaintiff entertained no vindictive feelings towards the defendants, and authorised them to offer that if the defendants would pay the costs and apologise, no further litigation should follow.

Mr. Anderdon (with Mr. Shebbeare) declined to enter into any arrangement. The plaintiff must take his remedy at law.

His Honour said that he considered it would be more prudent and safe to narrow the present injunction, than leave in words susceptible of an erroneous impression. The plaintiff could, without prejudice to his injunction, amend his bill, or file a supplemental bill, or take any other course he might be advised. At present the words "or imitate" must be struck out. He should therefore vary the injunction by erasing these words. The defendant requiring the plaintiff to be put upon terms to bring an action, and the Court, at the defendant's request, requiring the plaintiff to bring that action, let the plaintiff, within ten days, bring an action against the defendants for the invasion of his alleged copyright, and prosecute the same with due diligence, the plaintiff undertaking to abide by any order that the Court might make after the trial of the action.

DICKENS'S SECOND APPEARANCE IN CHANCERY.

Bradbury v. *Dickens.*

(27 Beavan, 53.)

The facts as disclosed by the Report are as follows: By agreement of the 28th of March 1850, it was provided that *Household Words* should be established, Dickens taking half the profits, Bradbury and Evans one-fourth, and Forster and William Henry Wills the remaining fourth. Dickens was to be editor, and to exercise absolute control over the literary department. In consequence of misunderstandings, he, on the 22nd of December 1858, gave notice to dissolve the partnership in the following May, and he advertised the forthcoming appearance of *All the Year Round.* This advertisement included an "Address," in which he spoke of transferring himself and his strongest energies from the publication that was about to be discontinued to the publication that was about to begin. The address ended as follows: "On Saturday, 28th May 1859, Mr. Charles Dickens will cease to conduct *Household Words*, that periodical will be discontinued, and its partnership of proprietors dissolved."

Bradbury & Evans filed a bill in Chancery against Dickens and Wills (Forster's interest having, presumably, become vested in some, or one, of his co-partners), which bill prayed, among other things, that Dickens might be restrained from advertising the discontinuance of *Household Words*, or the substitution of any periodical in its place; and on the 26th of March 1856, a motion for this injunction was made to Sir John Romilly, the Master of the Rolls. Roundell Palmer and Jessel were the plaintiff's counsel. They contended that the title of *Household Words* was part of the partnership assets, and that Dickens had no right to appropriate it to himself, or to damage the continuity, goodwill, or succession of the publication, it being his duty on the dissolution of the partnership to make the most of the partnership property and rights. Selwyn and Hobhouse, on Dickens's behalf, argued that the full title of the periodical was "*Household Words*, a Weekly Journal conducted by Mr. Charles Dickens," and this being so, and Dickens having absolute control over the literary department, there was nothing not strictly true in the statements that he was ceasing to conduct *Household Words*, and that the periodical would be discontinued and its partnership of proprietors dissolved.

The Master of the Rolls decided that the title of the periodical was *Household Words*, and that the same forming part of the partnership assets, must be sold for the benefit of the partners. In his Honour's opinion the insertion of the words "by me," or "by the editor" after the word "discontinued" would make the advertisement free from all cavil. Accordingly, upon Dickens's undertaking to insert in future advertisements the words "by him," or their equivalent, no order was made upon the motion.

The report goes on to state that on the 28th April 1859, a sale was ordered of the right to use the name *Household Words*, and to publish under that name any periodical or other work, whether in continuance of the then existing *Household Words*, or otherwise, as the purchaser should think fit, and we are told in a footnote that the right was accordingly sold by auction on the 16th May 1859 for £3550, whereupon the publication of *Household Words* ceased. The purchaser was, of course, Dickens.

EXTRACTS FROM *THE TIMES* REFERRING TO THE ALTERATION IN THE ROLLS COURT HOURS.

"*The Times*," *Friday*, 19*th June* 1829.

The Master of the Rolls has announced his intention of holding the Sittings of his Court generally in the morning, instead of in the evening, as has hitherto been the custom for him and his predecessors to do. His Honour has at the same time intimated to the King's Counsel practising in the Courts of Equity, his wish that such of them as elect to practise in his Court will notify their intention to his secretary.

The following is the list of sittings which his Honour has appointed for the ensuing term and the sittings after it; the effect of which will be, to bring into practice some of the most important objects of the bill "for facilitating the Administration of Justice in Courts of Equity," which was recently withdrawn from the House of Commons, after having passed the Lords.

At the Rolls.

On Thursday, June 18, at 11 o'clock, on petitions.

At Westminster.

On Monday, the 22nd, and on every Monday, Tuesday, and Wednesday, during the term, at 11 o'clock, on causes, further directions, and exceptions. On every Friday during term, at the same hour, on consent, causes and petitions. On the day after the last seal, at 11 o'clock; and at the same hour on the subsequent day or days, if necessary, for the disposal of petitions, on petitions. And afterwards, on one or more days, as may be necessary, at 9 o'clock, on consent, causes and petitions.

"*The Times*," *Monday, the* 22*nd June* 1829.

Law Report.

Court of Chancery, Saturday, June 20.

The Master of the Rolls sits on Monday at Westminster in the Court of Chancery. The Lord Chancellor will be at the House of Lords on that day.

"*The Times,*" *Tuesday, 23rd June* 1829.

LAW REPORT

ROLLS' COURT, MONDAY, JUNE 22.

The Master of the Rolls held his Court in one of the Committee Rooms of the House of Commons (No. XIII). His Honour disposed of his list of cause petitions, and heard some trifling matters of no public interest.

His Honour intimated to the bar that his medical advisers were of opinion it was by no means certain he would be able to go through with the arrangement he had made for morning sittings. He therefore wished them to consider themselves at liberty as to their attendance in his court.

Note.—It appears by Tamlyn's Reports, p. xiii, that down to 1831 (the date of publication of the author's first and only volume) there had been no return to the practice of sitting at night. By this date the new order of things had, no doubt, become permanent, and I have not found any evidence showing, or suggesting, that the night sittings were ever resumed. It will be observed from *The Times* report of the 23rd of June 1829, that the Master of the Rolls' first sitting at Westminster was in Committee Room XIII of the House of Commons. From Soane's plan of Westminster Hall and its surroundings in 1795, it appears that certain rooms and offices of the old House of Commons then stood north of Old Palace Yard, upon part of the site which Soane afterwards covered. It is, therefore, not improbable that a portion of the upper part of his buildings was designed for the like uses, and that Committee Room XIII of 1829 became the permanent court of the Master of the Rolls. I am informed by a person who knew the court well that it was of good size, and looked out upon St. Margaret's Church.

THE GREAT COURT OF EXCHEQUER, QUEEN ELIZABETH'S CHAMBER, &c.

EXTRACTS FROM SOANE AND OTHER WRITERS.

In July 1820, I was directed by the Lords Commissioners of His Majesty's Treasury to prepare plans for the New Law Courts. . . . The Plans for the Courts being completed . . . were submitted to the Lords of the Treasury. . . . Various improvements were . . . made in the Plans from time to time, to the satisfaction of the Judges of the different Courts, and to many of the Gentlemen of the Bar, to whom they were shown. Several weeks were occupied in making these arrangements, and during that time a large portion of the old Court of Exchequer, erected in the time of Queen Elizabeth, and the Rooms under the Court for the Records, proposed by my plan to be left *in statu quo*, had been pulled down. . . .—(Soane's *A Brief Statement of the Proceedings respecting the New Law Courts at Westminster, &c.* (1828), p. 182.)

The ancient *Court of Exchequer*, which had probably been founded as early as Henry the Third's reign, but was greatly altered in the time of Queen Elizabeth (and the site of which is now occupied by the Bail Court, &c.), was 74 feet in length and 45 feet in width. Adjoining it, southwards, was the Little Exchequer Court, which had also the traditional name of Queen Elizabeth's Chamber. The lower apartments, beneath each of these Courts, had been for a long time appropriated to the storage of records; and several smaller offices, westward (all of which have been destroyed), were used for similar purposes.—(Brayley & Britton's *History of the Ancient Palace . . . at Westminster* (1836), p. 462.)

The ancient apartment known as the Court of Exchequer, 74 feet long and 45 in breadth, was probably built in the reign of Edward II. The walls were 4 feet thick, ornamented with a corbel table; and formed within into such deep recesses that the windows appeared like oriels, 8 feet broad and 15 feet in height; the architecture being of that most pure and elegant period of the art. In the time of Queen Elizabeth only one of these windows escaped the touch of the miserable taste of the age, which destroyed their ancient symmetry, converting them into the debased Tudor style. Upon the bases of some of the pillars in the Chamber was cut the date A.D. 1570, this Queen having repaired or partly rebuilt the building after a great fire. This apartment, according to tradition, was the breakfast-room of that Princess, wherein she also diverted herself by hearing concerts. Over the gallery, in which the musicians played, was a long room filled with records, and said to have been the nursery of King Edward VI in the reign of King Henry VIII. One arch, close to the wall of the Hall, and of the same date as that fabric, formed the entrance into an oblong apartment, recently used by the Judges, about 43 feet in length and 29 in breadth, but rendered irregular by the projection of one of the flying-buttresses of the Hall into it; and this was, it is said, Queen Elizabeth's bed-chamber.—(*Westminster*, by Mackenzie E. C. Walcott, 1849, p. 217.)

No sooner, however, was Elizabeth on the throne than the business of the courts at once revived. "The spaniels came into the field," as it was said, "when there was plenty of game," and the roll of serjeants and of counsel rapidly increased. Westminster Hall and the Courts of Law became places of common resort; the Queen habitually occupying the Palace of Westminster, had a set of apartments adjoining the Hall with a spacious and decorated bedroom facing the Abbey. She used the great Court of Exchequer from time to time as a ballroom, and the gallery for a chamber of music. The chestnut pillars of the court were restored by her in 1570, when the chief officers of state, Sir Nicholas Bacon, the Lord Keeper; Dudley, Earl of Leicester, Master of the Horse; William Cecil, Principal Secretary to the Queen; William Paulet, Marquis of Winchester, Treasurer of England; Walter Mildmay, Kt., Chancellor of the Exchequer; and James Dyer, Kt., Chief Justice of the Bench, had their names carved on the bases of the columns supporting the gallery.—(F. A. Inderwick's *The King's Peace* (1895), pp. 187, 188.)

DICKENS AND THE BLACKING FACTORY.

"He could hardly have been more than twelve years old when he left the place." So says Forster in Chapter II of Part I of the *Life*, but it has now been ascertained that Dickens—who was born, be it remembered, on the 7th of February 1812—had turned twelve before his servitude began.

The Marshalsea Register of Committals and Discharges puts the matter beyond all question. This record shows that instead of John Dickens's committal having taken place some time in 1822, as Forster supposed, the date was the 20th of February 1824. It also shows that the discharge was on the 28th of the following May, the whole period of the imprisonment having been only three months and eight days.

This information, coupled with the undoubted fact that John Dickens was in the Marshalsea when his son entered the blacking factory, proves that Forster was mistaken in believing that the child was "turned at the age of ten into a labouring hind"; and, incidentally, the new evidence tends to show that the period of his employment was much shorter than the *Life* suggests. For reasons which are too lengthy to be set out here, I doubt whether this period exceeded a few months.

The Marshalsea Register is in the Public Record Office, where anyone can inspect it on payment of a shilling. The process of tracing its whereabouts was so curious that I find it hard to resist the temptation of setting out the particulars. This note, however, is no place for such details.

The following extract from the *London Gazette* of the 4th of May 1824 (p. 731), shows how John Dickens obtained his release:

> INSOLVENT DEBTORS COURT OFFICE,
> NO. 33 LINCOLN'S INN FIELDS.
>
> Petitions of Insolvent Debtors to be heard at Justice Hall, in the Old Bailey London on Thursday the 27th day of May 1824 at nine o'clock in the Forenoon.
>
> Dickens John (sued as John Dickins) formerly of Portsmouth Hants, afterwards of Chatham Kent, then of Bayham Street Camden-town Middlesex and late of Gower Street North in the same County, a Clerk in the Navy-Pay-Office.

It will be observed that the discharge was one day after the date fixed for the hearing of the petition. Readers of *David Copperfield* will remember that there was the like interval when Micawber was set free. We are told that he returned to captivity "when his case was over, as some fees were to be settled, and some formalities to be observed, before he could be actually released." We are also told that the prison club "received him with transport, and held an harmonic meeting that evening in his honour."

Printed by BALLANTYNE, HANSON & Co.
at Paul's Work, Edinburgh